'Soul-baring'                                    *The Washington Post*

'Immensely inspiring and candid … This bittersweet and poignant work will leave readers in awe'                    *Publishers Weekly*

'Williams's cool rasp leaps off every page, his story told in the direct yet impassioned language that defined his greatest characters'                                    *Vulture*

'A bittersweet memento of a generational talent gone too soon'                                    *Kirkus Reviews*

'A gripping, revelatory memoir'                                    *NPR*

SCENES

FROM

MY LIFE

Michael K. Williams was an Emmy-nominated actor and producer. One of his generation's most respected and acclaimed talents, Williams was best known for his roles on *The Wire* and *Boardwalk Empire*. He died in his native Brooklyn, New York, on 6 September 2021.

Jon Sternfeld is a former editor, the author of Unprepared and the co-author of *Crisis Point* with Senators Tom Daschle and Trent Lott, *A Stone of Hope* with Jim St. Germain and *A Forever Family* with Rob Scheer, among other nonfiction books.

# SCENES FROM MY LIFE

*A MEMOIR*

## MICHAEL K. WILLIAMS

*with*

## JON STERNFELD

PAN BOOKS

First published 2022 by Crown,
an imprint of Random House.

First published in the UK 2022 by Macmillan

This paperback edition published 2023 by Pan Books
an imprint of Pan Macmillan
The Smithson, 6 Briset Street, London ECIM 5NR
*EU representative:* Macmillan Publishers Ireland Ltd, 1st Floor,
The Liffey Trust Centre, 117–126 Sheriff Street Upper,
Dublin 1, DOI YC43
Associated companies throughout the world
www.panmacmillan.com

ISBN 978-1-0350-0955-8

Copyright © Freedome Productions, Inc., 2022

The right of Michael K. Williams to be identified as the
author of this work has been asserted by him in accordance
with the Copyright, Designs and Patents Act 1988.

1 3 5 7 9 8 6 4 2

A CIP catalogue record for this book is available from the British Library.

Printed and bound by CPI Group (UK) Ltd, Croydon, CRO 4YY

Visit **www.panmacmillan.com** to read more about all our books
and to buy them. You will also find features, author interviews and
news of any author events, and you can sign up for e-newsletters
so that you're always first to hear about our new releases.

For the men and women
who never got to be children

and for the children who
never got to feel love

# CONTENTS

# CO-AUTHOR'S NOTE

*We all are works in progress. Everybody
is a work in progress.*

*—Michael Kenneth Williams*

MICHAEL K. WILLIAMS—MIKE, TO THOSE WHO KNEW him—died on September 6, 2021, a few weeks before we were due to turn in this manuscript. He and I had been working for two and a half years on various drafts and iterations of this book, which began as one thing and gradually evolved into another. After his passing, the book was completed off of the extensive interviews he gave me.

Mike was open to sharing his personal story and experiences because he thought his journey, his openness itself, could offer solace to others. He was adamant that the book he wanted to write shouldn't be about self-glorification but was instead an honest chronicle of what he'd been through and how it informed the man he became.

He wouldn't want to hide the fact of what killed him—his addiction—and he spoke openly about the daily struggle the disease was for him and for so many others. There are references in this book to how he thought he was one false move from having it all slip away, about the fragility of life, and how it all could be snatched away at any moment: these are all directly from him. This is how Mike felt and how he spoke.

Early on in the process, he finished telling me an embarrassing story connected to his drug use and I asked if he was okay with putting it in the book. "Yes, definitely," he said. "I don't think I have the liberty of leaving that out." *The liberty of leaving that out.* It told me so much about him—how he felt his struggles had to be about something more than just himself. How he suffered and how it was not in his nature to deprive anyone who might benefit from the sharing of that suffering. He knew how pain kept inside multiplies and how pain shared subtracts. This idea would come up again and again in our work.

Sometimes my phone would ring and it would be Mike in a frenzy, that deep and raspy baritone, excited about some news piece he saw on television, some kid who had crossed his path, or some memory that had sprung up. He'd tear up retelling a story and his voice would catch and the pain would find a way to settle. Then he'd get worked up about something else and his voice would go up an octave and he'd find his way back down before moving on. He had so much love, passion, hunger, and ideas that sometimes it all just spilled out of him and you had no choice but to just let it flow and marvel at it.

Mike had an indomitable spirit and gracious energy, and I'm not sure where it all came from. On some calls with me, he'd be out on the street and I could hear strangers walk up to him and just start talking. He was always friendly, knowing that exchange was real for them, that it mattered to them. So it mattered to him. It was never a burden, being a recognizable face in the community. It wasn't the fame that fueled him but that connection. He knew he was playing a part. And in his final years, he had grown more and more comfortable with the responsibilities and the possibilities that came with that part.

His friend and activist partner Dana Rachlin told me that Mike understood that his greatest role was not Omar Little or Chalky White but being a community member and doing "the work," partnering with and mattering in young people's lives. And he grabbed it with both hands. In the week before his passing, he was in a really good place: optimistic, positive, energized. He was reminiscing to me about his old theater days and talking about his community work with that insatiable energy that was uniquely him.

Mike was open to the world in a way few are. As we age we tend to close off for protection, but Mike did the opposite. He wanted people to see in, and because of that he was open to other forces getting in as well. It was like he didn't have a layer of protective skin. It was a blessing and, sometimes, a curse.

When I think of Mike, I think of that line from Terence, the Roman playwright: "I am human, and I think nothing human is alien to me." That was Mike. Nothing was foreign to him, whether it was what was in people's hearts, their needs, their dreams, or their fears. Wherever

# INTRODUCTION

*We cannot make good decisions from a distance. . . . If you are not proximate, you cannot change the world.*

*—Bryan Stevenson*

WAY BEFORE I WAS ANYTHING OR ANYONE, I WAS AN addict. That was my identity, what people thought of me, if they thought of me at all. Into my mid-twenties, I was on the verge of being discarded, like so many of my brothers and sisters who never got a chance to be something else. But through God's grace, I am still here.

Not a day goes by when I don't think how easily it could have gone the other way. So I live my life as testimony to that fact. The closeness of the ledge keeps me sharp. Taking nothing for granted keeps me honest. And letting each tough or tender moment drench me like water—that keeps me, me. I get through it all by feeling it all, taking it all in, and putting it back out there as honestly as possible. I still feel one false move away from losing it all. So I do what I can in the time that I have.

When I say I can't forget where I came from, I don't mean that casually, like *yeah, you know, deep down I'm still just a kid from the projects*. I mean it literally: I *cannot* forget. It is impossible for me to remove that Mike from this Mike. We are all the same: The headstrong boy who wanted to dance, the confused teenager who didn't know who or how to love, the dumb punk who got his face cut open trying to prove himself, the scared addict hiding out from people who wanted to help him, the Black man who still feared his mother and missed a father. All those versions of me are tucked inside each other like those wooden nesting dolls.

There's no line that divides making it from not making it, because *it never ends.* I still wrestle with demons that won't leave me be. They never go away; they just get quiet enough so I can think straight.

I've been blessed to make a career out of doing what I love, but the environment from where I came, the conditions of my youth, the trauma that still lives inside of me, and the struggles that nearly broke me connect me with so many others. I want to tell my story not because it's unique but because it is not. We may each be fighting our own fights, but we keep going: that is what ties us together. Everyone who is left here has lived to fight another day.

This book is my effort to reach out to those who are the same color as me and those who couldn't look more different; those who are too young to carry all their pain and those who are weak from having to carry it for so long. I hope that by telling my story, by sharing my doubts and fears, my loneliness and some of my trauma, that I can provide comfort, maybe insight or connection, or maybe just the sound of another voice who *knows.*

It took me a long time to realize that "getting out" doesn't mean what I thought it did. I started to ask myself: *Wait, where am I going? Why is* leaving *the marker of success? Was I getting out or running away?* I couldn't leave it to others—mothers and police, mostly—to raise the next generation. It was my duty to leave breadcrumbs to help lead others out. Or else what was the point? Getting out only matters if you take your blessings, your hard-fought wisdom, your scarred humanity, and go back in. So I've spent these recent years trying to do that: to contribute any way I can, to do my part for the youth of my community, to bring light and heat to their stories.

All my pain has to count for something. If it isn't fed back into the community, used to help others find a way, then it was all for nothing. I mean, what else are we here for if not each other?

So I offer this book in that spirit.

*Michael Kenneth Williams*

BROOKLYN, N.Y.
JULY 2021

SCENES
FROM
MY LIFE

# CHAPTER 1

# THE CRACKS

**CLEVELAND, OHIO**
**NOVEMBER 2018**

"Mr. MICHAEL, COULD I ASK YOU A QUESTION?"

His voice was still a child's, but his tone had that grit, the kind that comes from experience. Daniel did not talk like someone with only sixteen years under his belt. But one thing I knew for sure: not everyone's year on this Earth is created equal.

"Sure thing, my man," I said. "Shoot."

"Okay," he said, leaning forward to be heard above the noise of the table. "Are you happy?"

My face likely betrayed me. Daniel was rangy and loose in the way of confident teenagers. And with one simple question, he had pulled my skin right off.

"Sorry, what?" I asked, tilting my ear forward. I'd heard him just fine, but I was thrown off. The smile across my face was for defense, honed over many years of self-protection.

But Daniel saw right through it. Maybe that's why he asked the question in the first place.

"Are you, like, *happy*?" he asked again, a little more hesitant, more like a teenager. Maybe he sensed my nervousness.

Daniel and I had known each other for only a few hours, but I was already struck by how this kid talked. When I met him, through members of the ACLU of Ohio, one of the first things he said was, "Yeah, I've been working to turn my life around." *Turn my life around?* What kid talks like that? What does it say about America that the life of a sixteen-year-old boy was already so far in the wrong direction that he needed to turn it around?

Daniel was from a rough part of Cleveland, a city that often had one of the highest murder rates in the country. "Too much death," he had said earlier, "a lot of friends dying. Or in jail." He lived one block over from the projects, and that closeness wasn't just about geography. He was teetering on the edge between two worlds, and turning his life around meant facing threats on both sides.

One threat was the gangs, and the violence that grew out of them. "Sometimes people in the streets are bullied and they need protection," he told me. "They're sick of being the one who's the victim, getting guns pulled on them, and they turn into the person that starts doing stuff like that."

"Yeah, I get it," I said. I remembered gangs forming in the Brooklyn projects of my youth. It felt like overnight it went from a rivalry between buildings and courts—kid stuff—into violent gangs. Some of them came together because they wanted to and some because they felt they needed to.

From what I could see, not much had changed, except each generation is starting a little earlier than the last.

"There's people younger than me that carry guns now, it's crazy," he said. "Fourteen-year-olds walking around with guns you'd see on an officer. And they're not little guns; they really got stuff." Daniel told me a story about how one night he was walking to his friend's building and looked down to see a bright-green beam, like from the sights of an automatic weapon, on his chest. Instantly, he froze. The beam lingered. He didn't know whether to turn around and run or what. Paralyzed, he just stood there. And then, the beam disappeared. When his heart stopped rumbling, he took off running down the street. It's moments like these—a fear that most can't imagine, a stress that doesn't just pass—that makes some people's years weigh heavier than others.

The other threat came from those who should be protecting him. Cleveland was actually the birthplace of stop and frisk, an excuse to harass Black and Brown citizens on their way to work or school. Daniel told me about times he was held up at the mass-transit station for no reason, handcuffed to a bench for suspicion of carrying drugs while all he had was a backpack of schoolbooks. Calm and polite to the officers, Daniel had had enough of these police encounters to know they were looking for a reason to escalate. Most Black men know this from experience—cops doing things just because they can, because it sends a message about power and belonging. It's a trap, because if you react, you just feed into it. So the best move is to be quiet, to take it, though every fiber in your being wants to explode. "I think it's all like a setup, man," Daniel said. "It's designed for you to fail out here, for real." He's not wrong.

He told me another story that just tore at my insides. When Daniel was thirteen, he and his friends went out to a nice neighborhood to trick or treat on Halloween. "Out of the ghetto and to the suburbs, where all the mansions at," he said. "Once you go under the bridge, the whole scenery changes." But a group of Black boys on the clean white sidewalks, knocking on the doors of clean white houses, made some people nervous. And people pay good money to live in places where they don't ever have to feel nervous. So neighbors called the cops—who actually showed up. "The cops told us we couldn't be there," Daniel said. "That we were in the wrong neighborhood."

I thought about that phrase—"wrong neighborhood"—and how it got twisted inside out. "Wrong" is what most people would call Daniel's neighborhood, as in *we got caught after hours in the wrong neighborhood*. But here, it meant the opposite—the kind of beautiful place that kept Daniel and his friends out. It was the wrong neighborhood for their skin color. When the cops rounded up Daniel and his friends, they didn't bring them into the precinct. They couldn't: there was no charge. So they just dropped the kids off back in the hood. *Where they belonged.* Over time, Black boys get the message. Every Black man was once a Black boy who got that same message.

Daniel was carrying two traumas: the loss of his mother when he was very young and the murder of his best friend in eighth grade. *Eighth grade.* Think about meaningful or memorable things that happened to you around that age, how you carry them with you, how they shaped who you are. Most people can't fathom what that kind of trauma does to a young mind. He's lost more friends to gun violence since then, and a childhood like that grows heavy, like a weight chained to his foot. You don't just run free with something like that attached to you.

So there was this rawness about him, this tenderness, like his heart was on the outside of his body. His question to me wasn't a challenge; he just wanted to know. *What does happy look like? I'm gonna ask this guy. He seems to be doing okay. Maybe he knows.*

Considering what I knew about this kid, his question had gravity. Answering it felt like a responsibility, maybe bigger than I could handle. I was ill equipped, especially at that moment, teetering on the edge myself that day. But I'll get to that later.

We were at dinner with about twenty people, sitting at a long L-shaped set of tables at a restaurant in the Shaker Square neighborhood of Cleveland. Daniel was the only kid there, invited along by the ACLU of Ohio, where he was completing a mentorship. At the table were members of the organization, along with members of the Innocence Project and social justice advocates from both Cleveland and New York, including NYC Together's Dana Rachlin, and my nephew Dominic.

It had been a heavy day, so by dinner that night, I had let my guard down and switched into off mode. But I was sitting across from someone who didn't have that luxury. When the dinner was over and we said our goodbyes, I could leave. But Daniel had to go home. So when he asked me if I was happy, I wanted to give him a real answer. Other people at the table must have sensed the energy shift because they stopped talking and looked over at us.

Now, I like to think I'm an open book. I actually pride myself on it. Friends know they can tell me anything, acquaintances tend to confide in me, full-on strangers walk up to me on the street and just start talking like we go way back. But maybe my openness was a front, a screen to make sure nobody ever got too close to the white meat. Daniel went right for it.

*Happy? Was I happy?* This kid didn't have questions about Hollywood or Tupac or *The Wire*. I knew how to answer those. That's just part of the job. But this? I was flying blind.

"Well, that's an interesting question," I said, stalling for time. Searching my brain, the voice of Reverend Ronald B. Christian popped into my head. Rev. Ron—the man who had saved my life. "You know," I said, "my friend once explained that the word 'happy' is derived from the word 'happenstance.' Which means things that are given to you. So when you seek happiness, its source is outside of you."

Daniel's eyes were locked on mine—not just waiting to talk, but actually interested in the answer. Young people are open in a way that adults never are. Show me a struggling man and I'll show you a boy never given a chance to change.

"But *joy*, he said, comes from a different source," I continued. "When you have joy, there's peace of mind. So you're content with yourself. And I always took that as my goal."

I thought Daniel might laugh at me or call BS. But instead he nodded, the words landing. "I get you, sure. I get it," he said, leaning back. "Yeah, *content*. I like that."

There was a beat as I felt the tension release. The moment had been a little too real, so I had to undercut it. With a laugh, I said, "Now, leave me alone, you little shit."

WITH ITS IMMACULATE WOOD floors and modern decor, the restaurant, Edwins, looked like a regular fine-dining establishment. But it was actually something of a miracle. Edwins Leadership & Restaurant Institute is a free culinary and hospitality management school and a classic French restaurant rolled into one. What sets it apart is that all its students are formerly incarcerated men and women of all ages.

Among the fine linens and haute cuisine were chefs and waitstaff and managers getting their lives back on two feet. The staff—including the front of the house—was overwhelmingly Black; I've been to enough fancy restaurants to notice that color, if there at all, is often relegated to the back. But this place was being run mostly by people of color, learning a trade, recharting their lives, and feeding their community in the process.

Brandon, the owner and operator of Edwins, was a tall and slender white guy with prematurely silver hair and deep-blue eyes. He came over to introduce himself and gamely answered our questions. He was forthcoming about his own history, which was directly tied to the restaurant's mission. When he was a juvenile, Brandon was facing up to ten years in prison when a merciful judge gave him a second chance. He grabbed that opportunity and didn't look back, building an impressive culinary career out of it, putting enough distance between himself and his troubled youth.

I respect Brandon for what he was able to do, but what he did next is what made me in awe of this guy. In 2007, he decided to offer other people in his community the same chance he had. He started Edwins, which opened its arms to those with felonies on their records, all those people who were having a hard time getting hired anywhere, much less being able to build a sturdy career. If you're willing to learn and put in the work, you're welcome at Edwins. The place spoke directly to my soul. I was sitting there that night only because I had been given another chance. And second chances—or even first ones—had been on my mind.

The thing that had brought us to Cleveland was a series of screenings of a Vice HBO documentary I had produced called *Raised in the System*. It tells two stories in parallel to each other. One is the story of my nephew, Dominic Dupont, who served twenty years in prison for a crime he committed as a juvenile. The film follows his transformation into a mentor of others behind bars, a guiding light to men twice his age. As a testament to his service and rehabilitation, Dominic's sentence was commuted by New York governor Andrew Cuomo in early 2018.

The film also follows my own journey to educate myself about the world of juvenile justice. I meet mostly Black and Brown kids whose lives were snatched away before they even had a chance to sketch out who they were. The juvenile justice system, which looks frighteningly like the adult justice system, had made that decision for them. I met kids facing serious time behind bars, other kids trapped in the cycle that kept them right outside those bars, and schoolchildren whose lives had been affected by a generation of incarcerated parents.

Though I had educated myself on the numbers—we lock up more children in America than anywhere else in the world—the flesh-and-bone reality cut so much deeper. Of course children need to be held responsible for their bad choices, but that's not what we're doing by locking them up. If we genuinely cared about that, we'd put the time and money and effort into helping them with making better choices. But we don't even come close to doing that, and then we punish them even worse when they repeat the bad choices. We need to find positive and productive ways to intervene in their lives rather than simply locking them up. All it does is devastate families, upend communities, and ensure that these kids become criminal adults as well.

So the experience of making the film had a profound effect on me. It transformed what I knew and how I knew it. And that day in Cleveland dredged up all those feelings. Then we went to dinner and this curious young Black boy started asking questions more personal than I was used to answering.

Daniel was at the age where he could go either way. He was stuck on the fence, just within reach of a system that could eat him up, just outside it enough to see another way. He was in a stage of adolescence everyone goes through, but a sad reality in America is that some kids are given all this rope to run free and loose while others are given just enough rope to get tied up.

My time with Daniel got me thinking about what society

calls "the cracks." In some places in this country, the cracks are a dangerous thing, the gaps through which you can fall in and get lost. But in other places, like Daniel's Cleveland neighborhood and the Brooklyn one where I was raised, the cracks are the opposite: *they are how you escape.* I've seen enough to know the system is designed to trap people like Daniel, imprison or kill him or at least keep him on his corner. If he somehow gets a good job, a solid family, a happy life, I call *that* slipping through the cracks.

The messages are loud and clear to young Black men and women that they are not in control of their future. So it's a leap of faith to tell yourself you are. But believing it can be that difference maker. As Daniel said to me later that night, "I just feel like nothing's ever going to change, but I just changed me."

Almost thirty years earlier, I came to the exact same conclusion.

# CHAPTER 2

# JANET

BROOKLYN, NEW YORK
1989

A BLACK SCREEN. FADE IN ON A DARK AND DAMP factory, drained of all color. Searchlights circle above; rain pools down the brick walls. A monotone voice beams down: *We are a nation with no geographic boundaries. Bound together through our beliefs.*

Flashes of lightning: dark then light then dark again. Across a floor of heavy machines, the camera moves, seeking something.

*We are like-minded individuals. Sharing a common vision.*

Then a figure in a corner, hunched over. The face of a teenage boy, dark-skinned and distraught. An earth-shaking rumble as a freight elevator descends.

*Pushing toward a world rid of color lines.*

Lights crash on the boy's wet and weary face as he looks up toward the sound.

———

I WAS TWENTY-TWO YEARS old when a music video changed my life.

After thirteen months in rehab, I was back living in my mother's Brooklyn apartment, the only home I'd ever known. Twenty-two years and I was back where I started. Though I was clean for the time being, no longer headed for an early grave, I didn't have much to show for my time on this Earth. Staying alive had been enough. Until it wasn't.

My hours were spent working in a temp position for a pharmaceutical company and taking business management classes at community college. But I didn't belong in either place. I was just going through the motions, living out my mother's version of what success should be. The template my older brother had set. Meanwhile, I was waiting for something—for anything—to happen.

There had to be more than just surviving; there had to be living, and I had this buried desire to find whatever that was. I just hadn't yet found the courage to seek it out.

By that point, my mother and I were ships destined to collide. We were getting on each other's nerves, on top of each other's business, and up in each other's faces. I had been putting off the inevitable, delaying whatever adulthood awaited me out there. Sure, I was still scared of her, in some way would always be, but maybe I was more scared of venturing out on my own. It's hard to say. All I knew was that I was floating in some kind of purgatory, until something showed up like a message beamed from the future.

Anytime I could get into that apartment when my mother

wasn't home, I was there. So in the living room I watched the MTV countdown, waiting for Janet Jackson. At the sofa's edge, I sat, ready to pounce. I leaned forward to peek into the VCR to make sure the blank tape was ready to go for me to record it.

Back then, before we had much control over what we heard or saw, the anticipation gave it this extra jolt. You had to put in work to find the music you wanted, especially if you had no money. You valued it more because it wasn't so easily available. And when it arrived, it felt like the fates answering you, like you'd snatched lightning in a bottle.

The television screen went all black. I bounded from the couch and pressed the record button on the VCR, stuck my ear to it to make sure I heard that whirring sound. Then I sprang up and got into position in front of the coffee table, feet on my mom's rust-orange carpet. Back straight as a board, arms at my sides, fists tightened, I faced the screen and waited for Janet to count off.

The opening shots of the factory, the ominous elevator, the scared boy. Then heavy boots moving purposefully down the metal stairs, stepping through the smoke. Figures dressed in militant black uniforms with silver buckles, black caps pulled down low. Not just a dance troupe but a platoon.

Then Janet's gloved hand: 5, 4, 3, 2, 1.

The snare drum kicks off like a gunshot, the groove of the bassline and the New Jack Swing beat that could've put a dead man on his feet. The dancers launch into it like they were sprung from a cannon. Limbs swinging in perfect synch, legs marching and gliding at the same time. They all turn ninety degrees as though on spindles: left, back, right, front again. A dance in regimented precision but fluid like water.

Finally, Janet's voice like a whip: *With music by our side, to break the color lines.*

Her voice is fierce but not hard. It's optimistic, proud—*declarative.* It lands with authority, and I trust her because of that confidence. The troupe behind her trusts her too, mimicking her moves exactly. In the sharp black and white, their colors and genders are all washed out, discarded, ignored. They are all part of a single voice.

The boy onscreen, who is now up on his feet, goes searching. His fear has shifted into something else: curiosity. He wanders the cavernous space, seeking out the sound that has broken through his desperate world. When he finally gets a glimpse of Janet and her dancers, the view is obstructed by a chain-link fence. Eyes never looking away, he walks along it, with his hand as a guide. The song is an invitation, like Janet is personally beckoning him: *a generation full of courage come forth with me.* The boy is no longer alone. He is far from healed—he will never be fully healed—but there's a glint in his eye. The world has made room for him.

I cannot overstate how important "Rhythm Nation" was to my lost and aching twenty-two-year-old self. It spoke to the man I was and the boy I had been. The pull was so magnetic, I remember thinking: *I am this boy.* And I didn't mean it as a figure of speech. I didn't know where he ended and I began. I too wore my pain and loneliness like skin. I too was desperate for someone to reach out. And I too was being pulled by an invisible force, by the same force that was pulling the boy in on the screen. I was seeing myself on the television for the first time. This was not a music video. It was a goddamn earthquake.

I HAD GROWN UP with cute, baby-faced Janet—she was my age exactly—as well as Michael and their brothers. Those songs were the soundtrack to my childhood. I'd sneak on my mother's wig and sing Jackson 5 songs like "Show You the Way to Go" into her feminine wash bag, having no idea what it was. The tube part looked like a microphone to me. I'd sing and dance in front of the mirror, pretending the crowd was going wild for me too.

But "Rhythm Nation" was something else. The statement of a grown woman, sure, but Janet had a couple of records out by then—records about independence, love, sex. But this was something even bigger. A call to action. A message sent from a place where I belonged, a home I didn't even know existed.

The dancing and the music were interconnected for me. I wanted to understand the dancing, to get inside of it, to inhabit it myself. This choreographed movement that was both so precise and so free. Since I'd been a kid, dancing had put me in touch with my body, connected me to this life force and energy. Friends and I used to choreograph dances in the hallway and perform for girls or family members. But it was not a proper field, according to my mother. Not academic or professional enough for her. Not worthy of *her* son. So the desire lay quiet in me. But it never died.

"Rhythm Nation" was a freight train that woke it all up. I rehearsed and rehearsed that dance, getting a little more of the routine down each time. Once I got the video on tape, I did little else but practice in front of that television. If I didn't land each move exactly right, I was in the wrong position for the next one, so it was all connected. So there I was, day in and day out. *Rewind. Play. Pause. Rewind. Play. Pause.* I damn near wore that tape down to nothing. Once I felt confident enough, I performed it for some people I knew. The response was quick—and devastating. They knew better. They watched me for a little and then keeled over. "You going the wrong way, Mike!" they said, busted over laughing.

"What do you mean?" I didn't even understand.

"You're going backwards. You gotta face *away* from the screen!"

I had been dancing facing Janet like a mirror, but to do a routine you have to turn *away* from the screen, as though you're *in* the formation. It seemed obvious once they said it, but what did I know? I swallowed the embarrassment and went back at it. I parked in front of that TV, annoying my mother who wanted to watch her shows, practicing before breakfast in the morning and when the building was asleep at night. I faced away from the screen and looked over my shoulder to get it right. I watched out of the periphery of my eyes until I could do it with my eyes closed. I wasn't a fan imitating the dance; now, I was *in it*, among Janet and her crew. It severed the division between us. The whole world drained away and I was among them. That's what first gave me the idea that I could do this for real.

Dancing along to that video transported me out the window of that fifth-floor apartment in the projects, out to the streets of East Flatbush, across the East River to Manhattan, and on to the wider world. It all came together on that screen: my Blackness, my fear, my loneliness, dance, music, performance—it was like an explosion. Years later I read an interview where Janet said she was trying with that song to reach out to anyone who was teetering on the edge. And if she could get to one person, it would be worth it.

She found one.

"Rhythm Nation" was like a line drawn. I could stay and rot away or give myself over to this bigger thing. It was a risk but not a fantasy. More like a dare-to-dream moment. The video spoke to my brokenness but, at the same time, separated me from it, *liberated* me from it. I saw that I could be myself and still be strong. Dance had long been part of my identity. It had been a form of expression when I didn't feel like I had any other. So it made divine sense for it to be my way out.

When I closed my eyes at night, I saw myself in formation behind Janet. That song and its video were a turning point, but I also took it literally: something I loved, that I had been good at my whole life, that I could make a living at. So I came to what felt like a natural conclusion, though it sounded strange aloud: I was going to become a Janet Jackson background dancer.

I would make it happen: move out, quit my job, drop out of school. I would join the New York dance scene, immerse myself in that world, and find Janet. Or she'd find me. I'd start at the fringes and make my way in, through all the concentric circles and hoops, until I reached her. It had never appeared so real, so close, as it did dancing in my mother's apartment.

The arts had always been a rebellion in my home, a mutiny against my mother. And it would be again. She would berate me for throwing away a good job and a degree for what she saw as a pipe dream. But I knew better. When something powerful reaches you just at a time when you're ready to hear it, you have to strike. So I did.

I was tired of looking at that scared boy in the mirror, the one who was convinced he couldn't be anything. I was young, but had already been through enough heaviness for a lifetime. That scared boy was always just underneath the surface. No matter how many years I put behind me, he was the voice in my head and the spirit in my body. I carried him with me wherever I went.

# CHAPTER 3

# PAULA AND
# BOOKER T.

**EAST FLATBUSH, BROOKLYN**
**1978**

"HEY, FLAT TOP, YOU WANNA GO FOR A RIDE?"

I didn't have to be asked twice. Mom and I were clearing the dinner table and my father was dangling keys in hand, inviting me along with him. I was eleven years old and this was a rare thing, so I would've gone anywhere with him. Even just up the street was enough for me.

Dad had to drop off the music equipment at a club down on Flatbush Avenue owned by our neighbor across the hall, Mr. Cotton. Mr. Cotton was like a Black Tom Selleck, handsome and suave with a thick mustache. He had style and business sense and was like Dad's running buddy. On Saturday nights, Dad would load up turntables, speakers, and milk crates of records into a moving van and bring them down to the club. It wasn't the kind of place, neighborhood, or era when you could leave anything overnight. So around three in the morning, he would go back out to pick it all up.

Mr. Cotton's club was a dimly lit underground spot with its name in flashing bright neon: AZZ. You don't forget a name like that. The building was a small loft space with exposed brick on all sides. It had an upstairs office area for the DJ, which hung out over the dance floor below. That was it, nothing more than an open room. No bar, no tables, just a floor, a bathroom, and a coat rack. It didn't look like much, not like any of the vast places I saw on TV with the multiple levels, glistening floors, and candy-colored lights.

A few people were straggling around as I waited on Dad to finish setting up. Looking up toward the DJ space, I could see he was taking his time, chatting with people up there, laughing and easy in a way he never was at home. I waited, mind-wandering and a little bored. Right when I was about to trudge up those stairs and ask when we were leaving, the lights of the club went down. In perfect synch, a record started playing.

It began as a pulse, less through the ears than the chest, like a heartbeat, followed by a wash of organ and a rumbling bassline. Then a wall of horns and the wails of a saxophone punching the melody. Underneath that was a rollicking keyboard, and holding it all together was a four-on-the-floor disco beat. The sound rose up and blanketed the entire place; there was this tangible shift in the air. By the time the song was up on its feet, and pushed to full volume, people had materialized on the dance floor. Through the door, a line of popped collars and flared-out pants and dark skin filtered in. Saturday night in human form.

I knew the song—"Love Is the Message," a breakout hit of Philadelphia soul—but not like this. The DJ was playing a remix where the instruments were more urgent and the song went on for what felt like forever. More and more people flooded in from outside until that room was packed tight. I stood up against the brick wall and watched the men and women rubbing bodies, sound and movement and heat all feeding off each other in this mutual loop. My eyes grew enormous. I was taken in by the throbbing energy, the sensuality of it all. It was like a revelation of this secret thing that had been kept from me. I was a kid getting a glimpse of the adult world, a hidden place that had been closed off, and I loved what I saw.

I wanted to reach out and touch it.

"Let's go, Schnuckle Head," Dad said, grabbing me by my collar. I felt the tug but didn't move, like the volume on him was down. "Hey, hey," he said, clapping in front of my face. "Michael, let's go."

"C'mon, Dad," I complained. "Can we stay just—"

"No, no, no. Up, c'mon," he said, pulling at me again. "Let's go. Your mother don't want you hanging here." I bet she didn't. That's why I wanted to stay.

"Yes sir," I said, taking my coat and following him out the door. When we got back into the van, I could still hear that bright saxophone line, which played in my head the whole way home. And climbing into bed that night, the feeling lingered—that sense of danger, not menacing but enticing. When I closed my eyes in the darkness, I could feel it in my bones.

THE NEXT MORNING, I woke to Mom banging around in the kitchen, clanking dishes and slamming cabinets. The noise flooded through the thin walls of my room. Mom's moods were like weather systems that blew in and out of that apartment. And from what I could hear, one had touched land.

Rubbing the sleep from my eyes, I came out to see her cooking up a storm and my father nowhere to be found—again. Just the week before, he hadn't come home after a Saturday night out. Mom had gotten an early morning phone call from the police station and had to go down to bail him out. When the two of them walked in the door, neither said a word, but the anger coming off of her was like a crashing wave. He went into the bedroom and closed the door and she went into the kitchen. I later found out Dad and Mr. Cotton had been busted picking up prostitutes. I was just old enough to know what that was.

So, when Dad wasn't home again, I knew to stay out of her way. My stomach rumbling, I squeezed past Mom and grabbed a Pop-Tart, the last from the box. "Out the way, out the way," Mom chided me, passing in a blur with a hot pan. "Boy," she said, stopping to put all her frustration into it, "*get out of my kitchen.*"

Sunday morning was when she cooked for the week. Her hours as a seamstress in Bed-Stuy left little time or energy for much else, so she'd prep the week's food before church. She'd pick up a couple of steaks from the market, pour some

Campbell's golden mushroom soup on top, add Worcester-shire sauce, Lawry's seasoned salt and garlic powder, chop up onions and green peppers, and wrap the whole thing in tin-foil to bake in the oven. That thick smell would waft through-out the apartment while we got dressed for church, making it hard to think. If she was in a good mood, I could maybe touch the pan. But that morning the heat was coming off her so I stayed away. I went into my room and got dressed for church.

"Let's go, Michael!" she yelled. "I'm not waiting for you, boy!"

I came out into the front hallway to find my mother as she was every Sunday morning, decked out like the Queen of England. She was in a pink matching skirt and top, with a camisole, and one of her custom-made wide-brim hats with a floral arrangement. Mom came from the Bahamas, where the British colonial influence—conservative dress and buttoned-up values—remains strong. Mom carried those traits and looked the part, but underneath was something else, something fiery and vengeful. You did *not* mess with her. And my father was about to walk into it.

On our way out the door of the apartment, he came through, glassy-eyed and a little disheveled. Not drunk, but like he hadn't slept. He didn't smell like liquor to me, but maybe Mom smelled other things on him. Dad had this smirk on his face and went in to hug her, but she put her hand up, shutting him down.

"Don't even mess with me, Booker," she said. "I got no time for your shit." My father was mild-mannered and always a little removed, off somewhere else in his head. Had he just come in and took his ass to bed, things probably wouldn't have escalated the way they did.

"C'mon, Paula," he said. "Don't be like that. Look, look—" he said, digging through his pockets. He found some bills and held them out to her. "Look, I've b-b-been—" Before he could even finish his sentence, she snatched that money and threw it right back in his face. The bills floated like feathers onto the floor. She didn't need his money—she was the one keeping the house running.

"What the hell's wrong with you?!" he said, bending down to pick them up.

Once he raised that voice at her, my mother shifted into another gear. She turned around, kicked off her high heels, and hightailed it back into her bedroom.

I knew what she was going for—that underwear drawer. She kept a magnum BB gun in there, which I'd played with, and a real pistol, a .22, that I knew not to touch. When she came back into the doorway, she was hot as fish grease, pointing that .22 straight at him. It was a small silver thing that looked like a toy, but I knew it wasn't. So did my father.

He jumped like he'd been stung and backed up like a scared mouse into the building's hallway. "Paula, you c-c-crazy. C-C-Calm down. You c-crazy, Paula!" he said, panicked, his stutter coming out.

I could see real fear in his eyes. Dad didn't know what she was capable of. None of us did. My heart started to beat through my tight suit and I just wanted to get out of there. Even if it meant going to church.

Once Dad was out in the hallway, Mom grabbed me by

the hand again and we took off down the stairs. He knew better than to follow or even call after her. I can see him now, wiping the sweat from his forehead with his sleeve, stunned into silence. I didn't look back, just hustled down the stairs at the end of Mom's hand, certain he wouldn't be there when we got back.

That was the beginning of the end for them. Before the month was out, my father would move out and get his own place in Brownsville. He'd stick around in Brooklyn for a few years, but the marriage really ended right there, that morning.

THE FIRST THING I notice is the glow. It comes out and grabs you.

I'm looking at a photograph of my mother from the early '60s, a few years before my birth. Her face *shines;* her eyes glint and her teeth gleam, like she is lit from within. Her cheeks are lifted as though by invisible strings. My mother is open to the world in all its possibilities. She sits next to my father; both are decked out at a white-tablecloth event at a club in Brooklyn. A place where they had to present as a couple. My father has a relaxed ease to his sit, while my mother is carefully posed around him, a slight lean toward him. It is up to her to fix the symmetry, to make the photo work.

She's in a scoop-neck green dress, sleeves in a knit pattern, and long pearls. He is in a nicely fitted dark-gray suit, perfect thick tie knot. Below his thin mustache is a lopsided smile, but I'm not fooled. I can tell he's not really smiling. It's not in his eyes like it is in hers. My mother smiles with her full, raw being, while my father smiles because there's a camera pointed at him. I can spot the discomfort of a man hiding within himself. I recognize the look because I know that face so well. It's my face too.

When my parents met in the early 1960s, my father was already married with six kids, all under eighteen, living in the Lafayette Gardens projects in Bed-Stuy. I'd heard that marriage was volatile, that things like chairs and ashtrays were always flying across the apartment. Word was that he went up the block for a loaf of bread and a carton of milk, met my mother, and never went home. The truth was definitely messier, but the casualness of that story, the easy happenstance of it, says a lot about my father. He slipped out of one marriage and into another, leaving wreckage in his wake. My mother was not a naïve woman, not by a long shot. I just think she was hopeful about who he might become. But there's an old saying: how you meet them is how you lose them.

They moved into Vanderveer Estates, thirty acres of high-rise buildings in East Flatbush, at the time occupied mostly by Jews and Italians. This was back when Vanderveer's most famous resident, Barbra Streisand, was just making a name for herself in the Manhattan clubs, back before the term "projects" meant poor and Black and troubled. Those who lived in those vast buildings were working class, angling for that step up. That's what the projects meant back then: housing preceding a house. When white people predominantly lived there, the projects were just an arm of the community. But across cities in America, as the Blacks moved in, everyone else cleared out. And when the color of the projects changed, so did the association. The people were no different—still just working folks trying to get by—but "projects" would come to mean separate, problematic. *Other*. The projects were limbs chopped off by mainstream society. So we'd end up having to create our own.

Booker T. Williams had been a father longer than he'd been a man, having had his first kid at fifteen. He was a hard-living thirty-eight by the time he met Paula, who already had a two-year-old boy. Five years later, when she got pregnant with me, he tried to convince her to get an abortion. She refused; in her late thirties, she figured it was her last chance to have the girl she always wanted. My father dropped that fight, though I can't imagine he could've stopped her if he'd tried.

Booker would end up with ten children by four different women. It'd be unfair to single him out for this, because this is what we knew: fathers disconnected from their children. I would be a grown man before I found the *lack* of abnormality around this to be so abnormal. Most of my friends were from single-parent and broken homes and a lot of fathers were out in the streets, whether that meant chasing liquor or women or something else they couldn't even explain. In the Vanderveer of my youth, we knew one family where the couple stayed happily married, the Lewises. No one ever saw Mr. Lewis even glance at another woman. He was a magnet for the neighborhood boys, who were always circling around him. We hadn't *seen* someone like him.

I hate to say Mom and I got the dregs of my father, but if you want to put it that way, I won't stop you. I was an afterthought to him, a way to end an argument. He looms large in my mind only in his absence, in the gap he left for my mother to fill. Not officially out of the house until I was twelve, he was always passing through, the man who resembled the shape of the hole in our lives.

My memories of my father are thin, like glimpses in passing—him rubbing my head, calling me Schnuckle Head or Flat Top. I thought of him as this locked box, shut down, guarded. There was something hard and unknowable about him. Kids learn, whether they are directly taught or not, and I absorbed things from my father: *Don't show them who you really are. Keep that person close. If you give them a glimpse, they'll rip you apart for it.*

My mother fought hard for that marriage, but you cannot drag a man into a life he's committed to escape. So I was startled that Sunday morning when she pulled that gun on him, but I can't say I was surprised. Not as much as you'd think. For one, he probably had it coming. For another, I knew that violence was *in her.* My mother was bred straight from warrior stock. Her first cousin was Lynden O. Pindling, who led the charge for Bahamian independence in 1973, became known as Father of the Nation, and was elected the new country's first prime minister. That stubborn fighting spirit was in Paula's DNA.

The Bahamas of her youth was a poor and segregated British colony, where she had to fend for herself. Her mother, Madie, was an alcoholic who moved to New York, leaving her five young children to be raised by her own mother in a single house in Grantstown, a Black neighborhood in Nassau. My mother was the youngest, "the runt of the litter," as she put it, dark-skinned in a place where that was just another term for ugly. Given second-class status in her own family, she was made to sleep on the floor while everyone else had beds. She lived in the shadow of her older sister, Ellen, who had a British name, a white father, and the light skin that gave her more power. And she used it to make Paula feel small, telling her how to act like a lady and warning her not to end up "barefoot and pregnant like Madie."

Mom absorbed the message. By twelve, she dropped out of school and went up the block to a lady with a sewing shop and asked her to teach her how to sew so she could get out from under her family. The woman took young Paula in as an apprentice and my mother learned fast. By eighteen, she had saved enough for a ticket to Miami and a Greyhound bus ride to New York City. Her plan was to meet Madie at the Port Authority Bus Terminal, but her mother never showed. Hundreds of miles away from the only home she ever knew, Paula must've felt dwarfed by the scale of the bustling city. Among the tightly packed masses of people, under the buildings stretching into the sky, most people might've thought about turning back. But my mother never scared easily.

She found Madie up in Harlem, living in squalor and in the grips of alcoholism. Though still a child herself, Mom got them an apartment in the Bronx and nursed Madie through the alcoholism and sickness that would kill her a few years later. On her deathbed, Madie told her youngest child, whom she'd left to fend for herself, "Baby, God's gonna bless you for how you took care of me."

Alone again, Mom moved out to Brooklyn, at a time

when the postwar wave of Caribbean immigrants was flooding into New York. Through the years, all of her Nassau relatives came to the States through Paula. They stayed with her and leaned on her, this child they had pushed aside. But Mom opened her arms to them, because that's what you did for family. They all stepped on her shoulders in order to get this better life: green cards, money, jobs, apartments. And she was strong enough to hold them. So I was raised by a fearless woman and I got both ends of that.

Mom's love was harsh like sandpaper, suffocating like a thick pillow. I had to carry myself according to her rules, which stretched from my language to my walk to my manners to my clothing, which was the front for a lot of our battles. From an early age, clothes were my way of expressing my spirit. I liked to dress up—red sunglasses, army outfit, cowboy outfit. Not for Halloween or anything; those were just my outfits.

When I was nine, I had this matching tennis suit, short pants and white polo shirt with a little crest on the chest. It made me feel special—and the summer I got it, I wore it every day I could get away with. One morning, I started to put it on again as my mom was folding clothes in my room. "Un-uh," she said, not even looking up from the laundry. "You done worn that every day this week. That's filthy. Wear something else."

"But Ma, I wanna—"

"Don't you talk back to me, Michael!" She looked up, her eyes burning into me. "Put on something else. Now. Or you can stay in all day. I don't care what you do."

Of course, the clothes looked perfectly clean to me, and I

was livid. She tried to get me to put on a shirt she had sewn. "What about this?" she said, holding it out to me.

"No," I yelled, "I'm a pick out my own clothes!" I huffed and stomped over to my drawers, picked out something else, and put it on.

"You watch it, Michael. I can make sure you don't go anywhere."

About an hour later, I came back inside for something to drink and I noticed she was napping on the couch in the living room. I tiptoed past her, went into the bathroom, and quietly closed the door. I opened up the hamper and pulled the tennis suit from the top of the pile and slipped it on. As I was turning the knob on the apartment door, she rumbled awake. "Michael!" she yelled, sensing my presence. "Michael, come here!"

Trapped, I ducked behind the big living-room chair. As I breathed, I could see its plastic cover moving up and down, making crinkle sounds.

"What are you doing, boy? Get out from behind there." I didn't move, my heart pressing into my chest. "Come out, I said!"

I stood up slowly, sheepish and terrified. When Mom saw me wearing that tennis suit, she just snapped. She grabbed me hard by my arm and dragged me to my bedroom. Then she threw me onto the bed, put her knee into my chest and just started whaling away on me. It went on so long and loud that my father had to come in and pull her off me.

"Don't mess with Mrs. Williams," my friends would say. "She's mean."

She wasn't like that all the time. Mom found a group of

women who took care of one another, helped lift one when the other fell. Watching them as a young boy taught me about the smaller communities that bolster the larger ones. I have warm memories of Mom sitting around with Aunt Sandra and Aunt Miriam—neither of whom were my aunts—drinking Absolut vodka and water out of fancy patterned glasses, laughing and telling stories. They didn't tolerate shit from men, had their fun without sacrificing their dignity, expected the kids to be well mannered and behaved or there'd be some hell to pay. We called them the Goon Squad: You weren't getting past them. If one missed you, the other would get you. "Get over here!" one would yell as we scurried past. "Got you!" They carried love, but also their own trauma, which made it hard for them to forgive. They learned how to mask their pain and I learned from them.

AFTER MY FATHER LEFT, there was a bitterness in the way my mother treated me. It was like she felt stuck with this boy who looked like the man who toppled her life. I became my father's surrogate, the well for her anger and the target of her violence. If I talked back to a teacher or did poorly on a test, I'd get a beating. If I didn't clear the table or wash the dishes, I'd get a beating. She'd say, "Michael, don't touch it" to the thing I had to touch. If she said, "Don't do that, don't go there, don't hang out with her," I'd be attracted to the very thing, go to that very place, hang out with that very person.

"Boy, you got that defiance in you," she'd say. "I'm a gonna have to break that spirit." In hindsight, I see that she just passed down what she knew, what she was taught. But it stunted me. Any of my assertiveness was seen as disobedience, disrespect, a threat to her authority. For a long time, it confused me about speaking up for myself. In my home, that was treated as wrong, and I internalized that.

We were Episcopalian and Mom had been taking me to church since I could speak. She taught Sunday school classes, ran Bible study, and connected the church with all that was good and right. So I tried to seek her approval through those things. I knew how to genuflect in the aisle, sit up straight in my itchy suit, follow along in the Book of Common Prayer, and bow to the cross when the procession came past our pew. From the age of ten, I was an altar boy because I thought it would make my mother happy, thought it might win her over. Him too.

"Michael, I'm a have to pray for you," my mom would say, gripping my face in her long, rough fingers. "You got that touch of evil in you." She taught me that I had disappointed God—that I was unworthy of his love—and I took that into my heart. Heavier than the blood in our veins are the stories we inherit about ourselves. And the older I got, the more that feeling of being unworthy grew. My father left, and my brother didn't want anything to do with me. God became just another man I was seeking approval from.

When I was young, I was picked on a lot in public school because of the way my mother dressed me. I'd wear clothes she made, things like a bow tie, vest, and short pants. In first grade, two kids jumped me in a bathroom stall, and in order to break free I clocked one in the head with my metal Snoopy lunchbox, cutting his face open. The next day, the father brought his son into the class. At the front of the classroom, he said, "Point him out, son."

As though in slow motion, the kid raised a finger at me.

"Okay," the father said. "Go kick his ass."

My heart jumped into my throat as he walked up to my desk and started to swing away on me. It hurt, but what hurt worse was the envy I felt: this boy had a father willing to protect him like that.

When my mother heard about the lunchbox fight, she put me into a private school up the block, St. Stephens Lutheran. The structure, the uniforms, the Christian grounding—it was all supposed to help wash away that defiance. And it worked for a time. I was bumped up ahead a grade and I remember feeling like I had impressed people for the first time in my life. But I had trouble with reading, and not long after I had to be put back in the previous grade, like they had made a mistake.

When I returned, mortified, my classmates mocked me relentlessly. "Oh, what happened?" they laughed. "You too dumb to be up there?" The taunting got so bad that I started acting out. If kids don't get positive attention, they reach for the negative kind. And I was no different. The last straw was in third grade when a female teacher bent in front of me and, like a knucklehead, I smacked her behind. That was the end for me there. The private school didn't let me back and I spent that entire summer grounded, watching other kids on the courtyard from our living-room window.

When I returned to public school, I again responded well to the change, even garnering a spot in the intellectually gifted class. But in sixth grade, right around the time my parents split up, things began to fall apart. I started to seek out that negative attention like it was fuel. One time I was doing hand painting in art class with Mr. Epstein—a handsome, soulful Jewish man with a thick Afro. Mr. Epstein asked me to go wash out the pans in the slop sink downstairs and bring them back. On my way down, I stuck my hand in blue paint and smeared it all over the stairwell walls. My other teacher, Mr. S., a chunky man with a head of curly hair that hung down to his shoulders, would often send letters home or call my mother. One time he called her in for a meeting.

"You're going to have issues with Michael as he gets older," he told her. "To be honest, from what I've seen, he'll probably end up on drugs at some point." At the end of the year, at my sixth-grade graduation, Mr. S. looked out onto the gym of twelve-year-olds and gave us his most uplifting prediction: "Some of you are not going to make it." I felt like he was talking directly to me.

My problem wasn't academic issues so much as distractibility. I was diagnosed as hyperactive, and a doctor prescribed me Ritalin, but my mother got a second opinion—from the church—and threw those pills out.

My troubles at school were always treated in opposition to my brother Paul, eight years older and everything I wasn't. Paul was the golden boy, literally (lighter-skinned than me) and figuratively: he was the well-behaved and proper student, the dutiful son, the good citizen. "My boy, my good son," my mom would say to Paul, patting his head, touching his face. And he'd sop it up like gravy to a biscuit. She called him Bun—short for Bunny—a pet name that stuck into adulthood.

Whether Mom realized it or not, she was re-creating the dynamic she had with her sister back in the Bahamas. I was her "black and ugly child," she would say, like it was a fact as certain as my name. I remember the first lotion my mother ever put on my face was a bleaching cream called Artra, to lighten my skin. My defiance, my darkness, my weakness—they were all fodder for my mother. I learned to perform from an early age, imitating what I thought she wanted to see, hiding who I truly was. But it was never enough.

What made the comparisons worse was how desperate I was for some positive male role model, and how cruel Paul was to me. One time, in the kitchen, Paul was at the table looking through a large encyclopedia.

"What are you looking at? What is that?" I asked.

"Come here, Mike, let me show you something," he said. I came over and sat next to him. He turned to a photo spread of skinny African children in the desert, dirty, with big eyes and hollow cheeks.

"Damn, Paul, where is that?" I asked.

"You know how Mom is always saying you need to behave?" Paul said.

"Yeah." Of course I had.

"Well, this is the school they send children to whose parents don't want them no more. Mom's gonna send you there if you don't listen to her."

"Nah, shut up," I said. "You're lying."

"I'm not. I heard her say so. She told me about how she

was gonna send you to the reform school. Make it easier on her."

I believed him. It seemed possible that Mom would want to send me there. That this was where I belonged. I didn't question it. It didn't change my behavior, but it put the fear of God in me.

Into my teen years, I was still looking for acceptance, for validation. And if you don't find it in one place, you're going to look for it somewhere else. The soul needs that. It needs someone saying, *I see you,* something that makes you feel alive. Even if that someone—or something—can take you down.

# CHAPTER 4

# THE VEER

BROOKLYN, NEW YORK
1979–1982

VANDERVEER WAS A SELF-CONTAINED WORLD, LIKE
a small city: fifty-nine buildings lined up like giant soldiers
across thirty acres of Brooklyn landscape: six stories high,
seven apartments per floor, 2,500 apartments for 12,000 people. As kids, everything at Vanderveer revolved around the
courtyard, which was more court than yard: a stretch of open
concrete and gravel abutting the buildings. The courtyard off
our building, which we called the Terrace, was raised up a
few floors from the sidewalk and ran alongside ten buildings. Up to a certain age, that was our everything: our backyard, our front lawn, our dance floor, our meeting spot, and
our ball fields. On that court you'd have your first victory,
your first loss, your first kiss, your first fight. Besides school
and church—and a few other places we were dragged to—
the courtyard was our experience of the outside world. The
world in one city block.

We were poor, and we had to invent our fun, but I didn't feel like I was missing anything. We didn't need the manicured fields of Prospect Park or whatever the private schools had—we didn't even *know* what they had—because we felt like we had it all. There wasn't the kind of exposure there is nowadays to worlds outside our door. We knew what we knew.

We'd play punchball or stickball, drawing strike zones on the buildings, or turn any wall into a handball court. We'd chalk out boxes on the concrete for hopscotch or skelly, getting on our hands and knees, flicking the tops of jars into boxes and knocking each other out. I came home with ripped holes and dirt on my school uniform and my mom would give me hell. We'd play football on the gravel—touch in the summer, tackle when the snow was on the ground. I have scars on my knees to this day from falling too many times on a field of no grass. I'd come home all roughed-up again, and Mom would throw a fit. "You think I got nothing better to do than sew and wash your clothes?" But of course I'd go do it again. That was the freedom of youth: for a time, pain was a temporary thing, and only skin-deep.

The happiest times in my community were parties we had on the courtyard, which we called jams. (In later years, we'd get permits to block off Foster Avenue for summer block parties.) The jams had the air of family barbecues. We'd wait until the sun went down, and people would set up DJ equipment or their sound system, spin records, and residents of all ages would hang out, dance, flirt, and laugh. Adults would sit out on chairs drinking beer and malt liquor, teenagers would sneak behind the staircase to smoke weed or make out behind the buildings, little kids would run wild. We all mixed together and put our worries aside and partied like a big family. The crescendo of the night was when the teenage girls would perform these African dances. They'd come out in brightly colored prints that my mother helped sew and do their choreographed moves while chanting in Swahili, or whatever it was. It was a sight.

"Remember when Deena's shirt flew up last time," my friend Maurice was saying. "And those titties popped out?" Maurice mimed with his hands, and everyone busted out laughing. Deena had filled out over the summer and everyone couldn't help but notice. Maurice and Daryl and I had grown up together and we were killing time on the outside staircase closest to my building while they set up for the jam.

"Hell yeah!" Daryl said. "She was like—*mama se, mama sa, mama koosa*—and woop!" I laughed along but didn't say a word. Deena's brother, Eddie, had walked up with a friend of his while we were laughing.

"You shut your mouth about my sister, or we gonna go at it," Eddie said.

Eddie was dark with a short peasy Afro. It wasn't his looks but his outsized spirit that made him attractive, to girls and to me, though I wasn't sure what it was at the time. My attraction to boys, my desire for acceptance, and my yearning for a male figure in my life were all jumbled together in my mind. It was confusing for me, and what hurt was that the boys whose acceptance I wanted the most picked on me the hardest. It was like they sensed my desire and punished me for it.

"Your mother gonna let you come to the park after the jam breaks up?" Maurice asked me.

"Nah, you know she won't," I said.

"Yeah, Faggot Mike's mom won't let him do anything," Eddie said.

Daryl ignored him. "We're gonna play ball against Sunshine court," he said.

"Yeah, Terrace gonna smoke 'em," Maurice said.

"Mike, you can't come?" Daryl said.

"Nah," I said. My eyes were on Eddie, who I could tell was smelling weakness.

"Shit, no," Eddie said, running his mouth. "Faggot Mike can't go nowhere. He's a mama's boy. I seen him with that bow tie on before church," Eddie kept going, doing a little duckwalk, "looking like a little penguin bitch."

"Shut up," I said weakly.

Eddie stepped right up to me. "What you gonna do?"

"Faggot Mike not gonna do a thing," Eddie's friend jumped in.

He was right. Looking up to our fifth-floor window, I could see Mom watching over me like a sentinel. My mother was the gravitational force that kept me close; I had to stay near that first staircase in the court so she could keep an eye on me.

"Faggot Mike can't go nowhere," Eddie was still going. "Faggot Mike gotta stay home with his mama. He probably still sucking that titty!" Eddie and his friend were low-fiving and laughing. Maurice side-eyed me pitifully. He knew I couldn't do a thing, that there'd be hell to pay if I did.

The rule of my mother's that trumped all others: under no circumstances was I allowed to fight anyone. It didn't matter who said what or did what first; if she found out I used my hands, she'd use hers against me. Period. Violence was so ingrained in her that it was actually a type of love in her mind. She felt she had to protect me at all costs and she understood that every time I left the house, violence was a vortex that could suck me in. So whatever it took to keep me out of it was worth it to her. Even if that meant she had to use violence to teach me not to.

But it was emasculating. She might as well have sent me out there with no clothes on for how naked it left me. I was labeled "soft" in a place where that was like a branded mark. Enough times turning the other cheek starts to look a lot like you're just asking for it. So, by thirteen, I struggled to figure out my place among boys who were as comfortable in their own skin as I was uncomfortable in mine.

I hadn't seen him, but at some point my brother Paul—who was around twenty at the time—walked up to Eddie and got into his face. When Eddie kept up with the "Faggot Mike" taunt, Paul hit him right in the mouth.

It was surprising; Paul was straitlaced and had never stood up for me before. When Paul went to hit him again, Eddie took off.

As he ran away, Eddie yelled back to us, "I'm gonna go get my daddy. He gonna fuck you both up!" That was enough to make *us* run. Eddie's father was a hard dude in a place known for hard dudes; he was an ex-con just out of prison who *looked* it.

When we got upstairs, Paul went into the apartment and

my mother stopped me in the hallway, where she was cleaning up. At the end of the hall was a pull-down chute that connected to the incinerator in the basement. People on our floor would just toss their trash near the chute instead of down it. The garbage would pile up against the wall, the smell would travel, and the rats and roaches would come calling.

My mother regularly used to say, "I refuse to live in the ghetto." It was a declaration of defiance, less about a location than a state of mind. She was willing herself out of there, manifesting a better life. Our apartment was humble and small but immaculate, with touches of class and refinement in every corner. There was plastic on the couch and colonial armchairs, a china closet with family keepsakes, a shiny cherry-wood dining table right when you walked in. Up against the wall of the living room was this grand oak-wood entertainment center with a library and bar and records and stereo. I don't have a memory in my life without that piece of furniture. When my dad moved out for good, he gutted that entire thing, taking each and every piece out. It was like watching an autopsy.

My mother worked hard to beautify her small corner of the world, especially as the neighborhood and Vanderveer got more run-down and dangerous. She lobbied the owners for rubber plants, window curtains, runners to hide the wires, light fixtures, and a big mirror in the lobby like you'd find in a Manhattan condo. On the walls, she hung up gold-framed pictures of Martin and Malcolm and landscapes, but junkies kept tearing them down to sell. She finally just glued those frames so tight to the walls that you literally couldn't get them off without breaking them. She had that Bahamian backbone; you were not going to beat her.

Some of the other buildings at Vanderveer were on their last legs: holes in the ceilings, leaking pipes, broken glass, urine in the elevator, dirty diapers in the weedy grass. Because it was privately owned, Vanderveer wasn't technically projects, but that fact actually made it worse than places overseen by the city. Each new set of owners seemed to care a little less about the quality of life of the residents. And after a while, some of the residents stopped caring too. If you share a narrative enough times with someone, they start to take it as their own.

"What do you need, Michael?" Mom asked me in the hallway.

"I was out in—"

"Boy, pick up those pants," she said. "You know I'm not raising no street ni**er up in here."

"Yes, ma'am," I said, lifting my pants by the waist. I was out of breath and panicked about Eddie's father, but she wasn't letting me talk.

"What's wrong?" she asked. "Someone picking on you?"

"Eddie calling me names again and Paul hit him and—"

She looked down and shook her head a few times. "Eddie C—? Eddie whose father's in and out of prison all the time?"

"Yes, and now he's gonna—"

"What'd he call you?" she asked, grabbing a dustpan. "Blackie again?"

"I don't wanna—"

"Nah, nah, nah. *You* came up here. Now tell me."

I looked down.

"What he call you, Michael?" she said.

"Faggot Mike," I said into the floor.

"Speak up, son."

I looked up. "Faggot Mike."

Mom exhaled in frustration. "I told you not to hang out with those low-rent ni\*\*as. Didn't I?"

I nodded. "And then Paul knocked him down and now Eddie said he's getting his daddy."

My mother put the broom against the wall and waved me with her toward the apartment. "Okay, okay, go inside."

From our bedroom window, Paul and I watched as Eddie and his father came around the corner to the front of our building. And then as they turned, my heart almost exploded: it was like the entire projects were marching right behind them.

"Damn!" Paul said. "They coming up here?"

"Mom!" I started to panic. "Mom!"

But she stayed calm. "Michael," she said, "unlock the front door and wait in your room."

"But Ma—"

"Now."

"You mean lock it?" I asked, confused.

"No, *unlock it.*"

I did as she asked and then went to my room, cracking my door to watch. She stood in the front hallway, leaning against the wall, left foot over right. And behind her back, in her right hand, dangled that .22 silver pistol.

The doorbell rang.

"Come in!" she called, sweet as can be. Just like a neighborly old woman.

The door opened and Eddie's father stood there with a wall of people behind him. A change went over his face as he saw my mother. He looked down at Eddie then back at her. "Ms. Williams?" he asked.

"Yes, that's me," my mom said with a tight smile.

Eddie's father turned to his son. "Eddie, what the hell you talking about 'someone messing with you'? That's Ms. Williams! Have some damn respect!" Eddie's father smacked him upside the head. "What's the matter with you, son?! Now, say you're sorry."

"Sorry, Ms. Williams," Eddie said under his breath. His father waved everyone out of there.

Mom never showed her gun, never took her hands from behind her back. She didn't need to.

My mother's power in Vanderveer was a force, and she'd attend those resident meetings like church. *How can we make Vanderveer safer? Who can we call? What do you need in your building? What do you need in your court?* It was like a second job for her. She was close with Mr. Clark, who ran the management office. He was a soft-spoken man from Guyana with dark skin and a fully manicured Afro. Classy and ultra-conservative, Mr. Clark was never without a suit and tie and always maintained this reassuring, calm voice. The loudest he got would be his low baritone laugh and then he'd say, in his thick accent, "Oh, Mich-ael, you crazy. Ha-ha-ha."

I'd go by that first-floor office and see him meeting with my mother and the owners, Hasidic gentlemen in thick beards with wide-brim hats and black wool coats—even in summer. The fluorescent lights in there made their white skin look that much whiter to my young eyes. The only interaction I had with any of them was on the first of the month when I'd hand our rent check through the office window. One of their wives or daughters would take it from me, without a word or eye contact between us.

In the Brooklyn of my youth, the Orthodox Jews and the Blacks were right on top of each other but occupying different worlds. At Vanderveer, the dynamic between the two was volatile. The owners had to hire security to walk them around the grounds or even just from their car because residents confronted them about the state of their apartments and buildings. Mr. Clark was stuck in the middle—he had to hire some ex-cons in the building as his own security—but he never lost his cool with anyone. He could seamlessly switch back and forth between both worlds, never giving in entirely to either side. This made him a fucking superhero as far as I was concerned.

I don't remember East Flatbush ever being white, but I have clear memories of it going from an African American community to a Caribbean immigrant community. In what felt like a blink, Nostrand Avenue between Avenue D and Foster went from entirely Italian restaurants to only Caribbean spots to, later, being dubbed Little Haiti. The new wave of Jamaicans and other West Indies immigrants brought their food (roti, conch) and their music (rockas, dub), but also a pride in their identity. Before hip-hop really put a stamp on our culture, I didn't know any Americans who were like that. We were just Black.

The flip side of all that spirit, however, was that it got

sharpened and used like a weapon against one another. Trinis didn't like Jamaicans, who didn't like the Guyanese, who didn't like the Bajans from Barbados, and so on. And nobody fucked with the Haitians. As all these different nationalities were moving in, the conflicts became about power and control: who was going to run the block, who was more dangerous, who was controlling the drug trade and which corners.

Even those of us too young to get involved in the violence still sopped up that energy. Looking for an identity for myself, I would try to superimpose theirs over my own. The Jamaicans were considered the leaders, the coolest cats, so that's what I tried to be. But Mom was Bahamian, and I was raised on calypso, which was like light pop music. It didn't have that hard edge or sexualized energy of dub or dancehall. Jamaican was like a costume I could wear to hide inside of. Just like at home, my energy went into pretending, performing, and trying to be accepted.

My father was from South Carolina, so I wasn't island enough for one group, not Black enough for the other. So I straddled both. Half the week I pretended to be the hip-hop b-boy, with the Kangol hat and shell-toe Adidas. The other half, I was *Jafaican*—stuffing cleaner's plastic into my mom's wool tam hats so I could pretend I had dreadlocks. I learned all the reggae songs, faked some patois phrases, and rocked the braided red, gold, and green wool belt and the Lion of Judah pendant on my jacket. The Caribbean kids laughed at me and the American kids just shook their heads.

Another reason I felt like I had to hide was that as my sexuality was forming, I also didn't feel like I belonged in one place. I liked girls, but I didn't know if I was attracted to boys too or was just seeking them out for validation. There was one older guy, Wayne, a Trinidadian with an Irish last name, whose approval I sought relentlessly. He was no Adonis, but he had this magnetic spirit that put him at the center of every circle. All the girls were infatuated with him and I was too. Wayne had a thick Trini accent, which was so contagiously melodic you couldn't help but imitate it. Once we were in a group in the courtyard laughing at a story Wayne was telling when he turned the tables on me.

"You nah respect me, Mike?" he asked.

"Nah, nah, I respec' you," I said, dogging a Caribbean accent, "I respec' you. You a *fine* specimen."

There was a pause and then they all busted out laughing. Wayne's friends were bowled over, hysterical.

"Yah making fun?" Wayne asked me.

"Nah, nah," I said, starting to flush in my cheeks, a little panicky.

"You calling me like, what, like an animal?" Wayne said. "What you mean 'specimen'?"

"Nah, I meant—"

"How ya so dotish, boy?" one of his friends said.

"He's a batty boy," Wayne said.

"Batty boy!" they all jumped in, cracking up. "Mike a batty boy!"

I knew "batty boy" meant gay, though I played dumb, not wanting to bring any more attention to it. I made an excuse to go upstairs to my apartment. I walked in, went straight into the bathroom, and just cried my eyes out. It went on so long that my mother banged on the door.

"What's going on in there, Michael?"

"Nothing," I said, straining to hold back. "Nothing, Ma. I'm fine."

"Well, you can't live in there. Come on out, now," she said. I heard her mumble something and walk off.

When I went back out to the court, I acted like nothing happened, because that's what I had to do. As a teenager, I was like a shell of a young man. I didn't know how to build myself up or even where to look to start. So there were two things I latched on to like a drowning man.

The first was music. Knowing all the songs, especially all the dances, had value in that world. The arts served as my communication device in a place where I felt like I had no voice. I played trumpet in the school band and at my graduations, performed songs with my friends, and learned all the dances I could to impress the cliques in the courtyard. The arts animated me in a way that nothing else did. For a time, they were a lifeline to a version of myself I actually liked, one that was neither weak nor scared.

Brothers Tim and Charles and I would use the hallways of Vanderveer as our practice space and studio for music and dance. Dean, a tall and stunning Jamaican kid, was our front man, and he would knock the girls right out with his falsetto. We would do choreographed dances and perform doo-wop like "Bubbling Brown Sugar," Jackson 5 tunes, or songs like Parliament's "Flash Light."

In the early 1980s, around the time of "Rapper's Delight," writing rhymes became the new thing. No one knew how to rap—that wasn't even a verb we used yet—but we decided to have a songwriting contest. I stayed up late in my room and wrote out my very first song in my school notebook, practicing and memorizing it. It was called "Picture on the Wall," in which a man reminisces about his lost love:

> *I saw your face*
> *on the picture*
> *on the wall*

At the time I was thinking of a girl in my class, but I'm sure my parents' split was on my mind.

The next day after school we performed for each of our mothers. Mrs. Brown flipped out; she was genuinely enthusiastic about all our songs, commenting on details she noticed in each one. I was feeling pretty good about myself when we took the stairs up to my apartment and performed for my mother, who listened patiently on the living-room couch. She complimented Tim and Charles and then turned to me.

"Michael, honey," she said. "Listen, you need to give it up. Quit while you're ahead." Tim and Charles thought that was hysterical, but I was quietly devastated. In hindsight, I think she did it to quash my interest in the arts. She didn't think it was sturdy enough to build a life on, so she just tried to kill it in its crib.

I was jealous of Tim and Charles, whose mother cultivated their interest in music. As we got older, Tim talked about wanting to DJ, and his mother bought him two expensive Gemini turntables and a mixer set, which blew my mind. She didn't have a lot of money, but she figured music was a healthy outlet, that it would keep him out of trouble. It wasn't about him becoming a big star, though he worked at it relentlessly and, not too many years later, that's exactly what happened. Tim Brown would go on to become Father MC, a big artist for Uptown Records (at MCA) in the early '90s. He was one of P. Diddy's first artists, and both Jodeci and Mary J. Blige sang backup for him. Watching Tim's trajectory was eye-opening. I saw that with work and a support network, it was actually possible. We cannot be what we do not see.

But to my mother, the arts were childish things. Beneath me, beneath *us*. "You get an education or a trade with your hands," she would say. "Go into politics or maybe the church." By the time I was in junior high school, she saw I was spending time with some troublemakers. I was more of a follower, doing what I could to fit in, and the kids with swagger were like magnets to me. I got into trouble for little things like truancy and jumping turnstiles, smoking weed on the train. I wanted to be liked more than I didn't want to do things, so I just went along. Just to fit in under the radar. My mom saw where I was headed and took it upon herself to intervene.

"You already hang out with these low-level ni**as," my mother said. "I don't want you going to school with them too." She falsified paperwork in order to get me into the schools my brother went to, places where she had relationships with teachers and administrators. For high school, I begged her to let me go to a performing arts school, but she made me go to Westinghouse, a vocational/technical high school, to learn a trade, because that's what my brother did. It had no art or music program of any kind. With that decision, the door was closed. She choked off the one thing that gave me a sense of identity, the one expressive gateway I had. And if those things can't get out one way, they get out in others.

By high school, I discovered the second thing to latch on to: drugs, which at the time meant weed. I saved up money from my after-school job, learned how to roll, and was always packing reefer for the party. Getting high—and getting others high—was a way for me to belong. It had the added benefit of letting me disappear from myself, which I craved. I started to slag off school, had regular run-ins with my mother, and looked for reasons to get high.

In the early 1980s, cocaine—and its cheaper version, crack—pushed marijuana out as the drug of choice, and the change in the neighborhood was pronounced. The gangs went into business with or against one another, the violence and territory disputes grew from that, and it flooded over everyone, whether they were in the game or not. Crack cocaine had these ripple effects that you couldn't help but notice. I remember seeing Mr. Cotton, my dad's old running buddy, give himself over entirely to the drug. Gone was the sleek and proud businessman I knew as a kid. He was thinner and grayer, like a wisp of his former self. It had only been maybe five years, but he looked like the life was just drained out of him. It was a sign of things to come.

By high school, everyone wanted to be *grown*. Playing ball in the courtyard was corny, doing well in school was corny. A few girls I knew were pregnant at fifteen, and the boys cliqued up with gangs, treating it like a rite of passage. What once felt harmless—bragging rights about whose block was the best, whose court had the finest girls—morphed into this violent, menacing thing, mostly around the drug trade.

At a time when all of New York City was unsafe, East Flatbush around Vanderveer got particular attention for being a dangerous place. Because of all the murders at Foster and Nostrand, the intersection right in front of Vanderveer, the cops and newspapers called it "The Front Page." (The cul-de-sac behind the buildings was called "The Back Page" because bodies would disappear there.) The first gang that really had a name around us was the Untouchables—the Touchies—who were made up of Jamaican guys a generation above us. The next gang, the Pay Hays, was my generation, made up of friends I grew up with. The kind of trouble my friends courted elevated way past what my mother would tolerate, so I opted out. But the violence leaked all over and I saw my share of shootouts and bodies, including people I grew up with, like Maurice.

Maurice and I had been friends since his family moved to Vanderveer when he was eight. His father was one of those project characters, a theatrical Southern gentleman, country as all get-out. He would peacock down the courtyard on Sunday in an all-white suit, with top hat and cane, a splash of red handkerchief. Maurice and I played stickball growing up, and sometime in eighth or ninth grade, he told me he didn't want to play anymore. It was that quick: one day he was there in the courtyard laughing with us, and the next he was down the street. The drug trade just swooped him right up and he went dark.

Maurice joined up young, and by fifteen he was already

muscle for his gang, putting in work for the crew. Younger gang members became shooters because they were more impressionable. Up to a certain age, kids are less likely to ask questions of the higher-ups. (I wasn't the only one out there looking for a father figure.) I came home a few years later and saw Maurice laid out in the courtyard with a bullet in his head. He died right there at my feet. That memory has never really left me. Sometimes when I close my eyes, I still see it.

IN THE PARLANCE OF *The Wire*, I was a stoop boy, as opposed to a corner boy, so I stayed on the courtyard. I was left to find my place among the younger kids and the girls. I was looking to belong, to feel like I mattered. And those desires—for a family, for a place where I felt valued—drew me to Joanie.

Joanie and I grew up together—her grandmother would babysit us—but around the time high school started, I decided I liked her. Thin with a bright smile and wide eyes, Joanie was not just beautiful but glamorous. Her mother used to spend real money on Joanie's hair, which was the most lustrous Jheri curl on the block. She was like a Black Joan Collins, dressing like a sophisticated woman: espadrilles, slacks, and blazers. Confident and authoritative and surly, Joanie was everything I wasn't. She knew who she was and what she wanted, and for someone like me, who didn't know either, that was like catnip.

That energy ran in Joanie's family. Her brothers were gangster for real. Her brother K— was the youngest of the

Touchies, and his name rang out throughout the borough. A good-looking kid with full lips and thick, wooly hair, K— was only sixteen at the time, but he had all the swagger of a grown man. One summer night I was with Daryl and some other friends on the courtyard staircase when a car pulled up on the curb. A voice in the passenger seat called out to K— in the dusk. He went down the steps and when he was a few feet away, we heard the shots. They were thin-sounding, like from a cap gun, but they were real. We all ran for cover, and I watched him stumble back to the staircase. When I looked back up, K— was just lying down, flat-out on the concrete. I thought he was dead; we all did. Fortunately it was a .22, and he survived. Joanie's family left Veer in a hurry soon after that and moved out to Far Rockaway, Queens.

Out in Queens, Joanie's mother fed me, let me sleep on the couch, and took me in as one of her own. I felt part of a family there in a way I didn't in my own home. Joanie had a handicapped brother and a grandmother living with her; her dad wasn't around, her mom worked long hours as a nurse, and when K— went to prison, there was a void in that house. I decided I was going to be the man that filled it. I tried to help out, do what was needed, but I became like the family's stray dog and Joanie and her friends' cuddly mascot. Joanie leaned into that power imbalance and she used to put me down about my physical appearance. "Look at you, all scrawny!" She'd laugh. She'd tell me I was too soft and treat me like a helpless little boy. I was trying to fill the shoes of the men in her life, the boys she dated and her brothers, but I just wasn't built that way. The gap was pronounced.

I wanted to impress Joanie so badly that I made plenty of stupid decisions, like spending too much money on her. My mom insisted I get a job at thirteen, before anyone else I knew had one. The job was sweeping floors for a tight and hot sweatshop in Bed-Stuy where Mom worked as a seamstress for Mr. Pete, a gentle old white guy with glasses. The job was mostly for me to stay out of trouble, and since it was the only way to get spending money, I was all for it. That was freedom: getting money of my own. But I was only so free. When I spent my whole first check on an Izod Lacoste shirt for Joanie, my mother was livid.

"You gonna take your money and buy someone else clothes before your own clothes?!" she asked.

"Ma, please—"

"You're getting that shirt back, Michael. If I have to take you over there—"

"Please, Ma, no—"

"Get your coat on. We're going to get it right now. I don't want to hear another word."

My mother took me to Joanie's apartment, knocked on the door, and made Joanie go get the shirt and give it back to me. "He doesn't know what he's doing," my mom said to her. I could see Joanie was embarrassed for me and I just wanted to die inside. I tried to do something adult and it backfired.

Joanie didn't care about me beyond her own needs. I was just another person for her to take from. In order to make her boyfriend jealous, she even took my virginity—an experience that was as forgettable as it was confusing. But it felt like what I was supposed to do.

# CHAPTER 5

# KENNETH

BY THE TIME I ENTERED HIGH SCHOOL, I ALREADY felt like damaged goods. Injured by my father's absence, roughed-up by my mother's hard love, and too meek to stand up for myself, I was a ripe target. After two men in positions of authority—one from school and one from church—molested me, I fell into an empty, dark state. It was like a hole I couldn't dig myself out of.

At the time, no one in our community encouraged us to talk about those things. Lessons about staying silent get ingrained in us deep, so that's what we do. That's what I did. And it ate me from the inside, hollowing me out, turning me into a shell. I was a teenager, scared like a little boy, weary like an old man. Already vulnerable and looking for someone to trust, I checked out entirely. I blew off school, got high all the time, and disappeared further into myself. Verging on suicidal, I damn near didn't make it. And I wouldn't have, if not for one person.

Joanie's treatment of me wore me down, so I started to gravitate toward her cousin Robin, who was alpha like Joanie but in an entirely different direction. Robin was a full-on flower child and lesbian, a beauty with cocoa-brown skin, hazel eyes, and natural hair down her back. In fitted Levi's jean suits and boys' shoes, she turned people's heads with her braless breasts pointed out like little missiles. Wise and mature, Robin was already dating women with jobs on Wall Street when she was in high school. At the time, I thought that was cool, though I now see how messed-up it was. She was taken advantage of just like me—she just carried it differently.

Robin taught me that I didn't have to be one thing, that people could be made of contradictions. She had a nurturing side that she revealed to me in private, but she also had the tough exterior she carried around Vanderveer. When I first met her, around when I was thirteen, I'd notice her eyeing me at Joanie's apartment and could tell she was thinking: *What exactly is up with this boy?*

The first time we actually spoke, she walked up to me while I was playing handball on my court. "When you finished," she said, "I need to talk to you about something."

I sweated through my tennis shirt. *Dear God,* I thought, *I'm done for.* Someone must've told her I was talking shit.

After the game, I approached her as casually as I could, hiding the fear in my bones. She was leaning against the baking brick wall, surveying the court with this air of relaxed cool.

"What's up?" I asked.

"Come with me," she said, waving her arm. Then she just walked off.

I looked up to my kitchen window to see if my mother was there. "Shit," I said, "I'm not—" But Robin was already off and down the staircase. I was still not allowed to leave Mom's sight, but Robin's confidence was like a magnetic force pulling me out of there.

She took me down to Brooklyn College, where her father worked as a tennis instructor. We spent the day running around the massive lawn like little kids and opening up like old friends, laughing and talking and playing hide-and-seek, smoking a little weed and sipping beer. I called her Pookey, and she started calling me by my middle name: Kenneth.

When I started worrying about my mother checking on me, I convinced Robin we had to go home. She rolled her eyes. "You can't be worrying about your mom all the time," she said. "These dudes going to eat you alive. For real. Don't you know where we live?"

I did. But my mother still scared me more than anyone on the court. She put the fear of God into me, and it took a long time for it to drain out. On the walk back home, Robin and I saw a wet piece of sidewalk cement blocked off with tape and Robin knelt down in front of it. "What you doing?" I asked.

"Marking the day," she said, like it was the most obvious thing in the world. She stuck her head under the tape, plunged her long finger into the wet cement, and wrote: *Pookey.*

"Sign your name," she said.

I bent down and wrote *and Mike*. Then she leaned over and wrote the year. I looked down to read it:

POOKEY AND MIKE
1979

She stood up and wiped the cement on the back of her pants. Then she put her hand on my shoulder, like a big sister, even though she was a year younger. "You and me gonna be homies," she said, matter-of-factly. It was like she was taking me on as a project. I felt seen, chosen. That was intoxicating, having someone pick me out and say: *you*. Maybe she saw something in me, though I think pity played a part. She could see I wasn't making it.

To survive in Veer, you had to be able to fend for yourself. As we went through our teenage years, Robin knew I wasn't a hard dude—that I would never be one—which was fine with her. But as long as I lived in the projects, I had to toughen up, if only to survive. She made a clear distinction between "out there" in the world and "back here," meaning Vanderveer. Even framing things like that was new to me, because I never really thought about anywhere else. I couldn't conceive of what "out there" even meant.

One summer night when I was seventeen, I was getting drunk and high on my own when I went out to the Terrace, my building's courtyard, looking for Robin. By then she had become my crutch, the person I could talk to about things that I hid away. Some project dudes I knew were hanging out by the staircase. One of them, Barry, told me Robin was out with Steven, a mild-mannered guy who was in love with her. Robin only got with women, but she would let Steven take her out and give her rides. He seemed to be content to just be in her orbit. Robin had that kind of power over people.

"You could chill with us, Blackie," Barry said. "It's cool." Barry was a football star, handsome and assertive. He was not mean-spirited—he liked to laugh—but he had a short fuse. I stayed with them, waiting for Robin to get back, drinking a little more, hitting the blunt they were passing around. I was blazed out of my mind by the time we heard the deafening rumble of Steven's car pulling up. They double-parked down below at the curb and Robin popped out. Even in the dark from that distance, she could tell that something was wrong with me.

"Hang on, Mike. I got you. I'm a bring some beer over," she said. "Give me one sec to look at this." Robin and Steven popped the hood of his car and were leaning over the engine, fiddling with whatever was causing the thundering sound. Smoke billowed out from the car's insides like a dragon's mouth.

The guys at the staircase started yelling out, heckling Robin. "Yo, we're heading out to Prospect Park later," Barry's friend said. "Everybody bring a girl. Steven, bring a girl. Even Robin, you bring a girl too!" The boys started laughing. Being gay was enough to be a punch line.

"Hey, Robin!" Barry yelled. "C'mon, let me smell your panties." Robin couldn't hear them, but he kept at it. "Just one sniff, girl. C'mon."

Now, I spent my teenage years feeling like my masculinity had been stripped away, like my nuts were clipped—by my mother, by Joanie, by hard dudes who stared me down or disregarded me entirely. In my inebriated state, I got it in my head that it was on me to defend Robin's honor. The problem was that I had no idea what I was doing and I picked the wrong dude to step to. Barry was the most ferocious fighter on that court. He'd been knocking heads out since elementary school.

I got in front of Barry, lifted my chin, and tried to pass on my hardest glare. "Nah, you're not gonna say that about my friend," I slurred at him. "That's not cool, man."

Barry looked around at his boys, and then stared me up and down. "You know what, Mike," he said, a knowing smile, "I'm gonna give you a pass. You're wasted, and I'd fuck you up too much. I'm gonna bust your ass tomorrow, okay?" He patted me on the arm like I was a little kid. Everyone broke up laughing.

All those bared teeth, glaring white in the night, cut me deep. It was worse than beating on me; I was so soft that I wasn't even worth the trouble. Without thinking, I just swung, like a blind man, somewhere in the vicinity of Barry's head. Nothing but the breeze touched his face. On instinct, he came back with a hook, that two-piece and that biscuit, and I was eating pavement. It all went black.

I woke up on the cement to a confusion of footsteps, yelling, and running. I found out later Robin came after Barry and fucked him up good. She hurt him so bad that she actually had to stay away from the Terrace for a while. The last thing Robin needed was my weak ass trying to defend her. She didn't need anyone to. Though Barry never messed with me again after that. In fact, his mother brought him to my apartment to apologize.

EAST FLATBUSH WAS VERY deep into Brooklyn, the second-to-last stop on the 2 train, and once you got out there, you were in an insular place, a self-contained bubble. In ways both comfortable and stifling, Vanderveer was like a little town. Those buildings were the boundaries of my universe, and my exposure to the rest of the world—even other parts of New York City—was severely limited.

From my roof, I could see the steeple at the top of King County's Hospital, where I was born. At that same hospital, plenty of people I knew took their first and last breath, never knowing any other world but those redbrick buildings. People really didn't even talk about other places except up the block and at the park. And it wasn't just geographical. There were ways to talk, ways to think, and ways to live. There were what women had to be and what young Black men had to be. For years I had been busting against the seams of the projects, but I had no idea what to do with that energy, that desire for something else. It was Robin who opened that door for me and showed me what was on the other side.

"Yo, Kenneth," Robin said to me one afternoon. We were smoking a blunt out on the roof of my building. We used to get high and then climb down on top of the elevators, ride them inside the mechanical shaft for cheap thrills. "You gotta get away from these small-minded ni**as. Come with me to the Village."

"Where's that at? That's that place down Nostrand?" I thought it was some underground club or something.

"Nah, dummy," she said. "The *Village*. Greenwich Village."

"Ah." I nodded, letting the smoke drift up from my lips. "Cool, cool."

"Kenneth, man. For real," she laughed. "You been living here your whole life, and you don't know the Village?"

I had no idea what she was talking about. Manhattan's Greenwich Village was only about eight miles from where we sat, but New York City doesn't work like that. Each neighborhood is a world unto itself and the real distance between the neighborhoods is cultural and temporal and exponential. Without Robin, not only would I have never gone anywhere, I wouldn't even have known there was somewhere *to* go. She snatched me off the block and, with a subway ride, showed me a whole other world.

The first time we got to Washington Square Park (which we called West Fourth Park), I was awed: break dancers spinning on cardboard next to boom boxes, street performers in the drained fountain, students and sunbathers and guitarists and conga drummers, skateboarders and roller skaters, the out and proud, the tattooed, hippie, punk of America all swirled together into one big pot. It was like all of New York City was lifted up by its ends and shaken and the ones who didn't fit firmly in place fell into Washington Square. I felt like I'd landed on Mars only to realize that I belonged there the whole time.

The park has winding paths that stretch out from the center like tentacles. Robin and I would spend hours drinking and smoking on a bench on the strip we called the runway, where the cool kids our age hung out. It was mostly the young Black and Latino gay community, looking fabulous, dressed to the nines, voguing, showing off for one another. There was some trash talk but very little actual fighting—it was playful competition. Robin was an accepted part of that world and I was like her little appendage. At dusk, we'd walk to the West Side Highway to watch the hazy sunset over New Jersey.

Nighttime was when it all went down. Robin introduced me to the downtown club scene, where dance and fashion and free expression and rebellious hormones and youthful energy and libido got all shook up and popped open like a bottle of Champagne. The look was very important: This was around 1983, and I started out with the high-top fade, the floral shirt, backward suspenders, and enormously gaudy shoes. But then we discovered our spirit guide.

The summer of 1984, *Purple Rain*—the movie and the album—hit like a lightning bolt. Prince arrived on the scene like a divine force from the heavens above. I am not exaggerating; his effect on me was majestic and spiritual. He conjured out of me everything my family and my community and my inhibitions had tried to bury. A hypersexualized role model and wildly inventive artist, Prince was part man, part woman, part alien. Small and frail in stature, he carried himself like the baddest motherfucker alive and held the stage like a fifty-foot god. And it all came from inside of him. He broke out of the mold of the shy kid from a dysfunctional household and invented himself. Instead of hiding his humanity, he wore his vulnerability like armor. I didn't even know you could be proud of your fragility like that. That type of strength blew my mind.

Around this time Robin and I fell in with this girl named Darlene. Darlene was dark like me, athletic, a stylish girl and sharp dresser who was also pushing back against her home situation. The three of us locked into this dress code for hitting the clubs: long black wool overcoats, thick black Ray-Ban sunglasses we called Mookas, and penny loafers, though we always put nickels in those slots. It was like Blues Brothers meet the Mod Squad with a Prince and the Revolution vibe.

The first club Robin took us to was the Garage, which was literally an old parking garage turned dance spot on King Street, just south of the Village in SoHo. The entrance was a giant car ramp with footlights along the sides leading up to the club, like boarding a spaceship. When we got to the top, the bouncer would slide back that curtain and we'd step into the club's purple light. As we entered, the back of our coats would be caught in the wind and flow dramatically, like in slow motion. We were teenagers, not even out of high school, but we walked into that place like stars, like all eyes were on us. I never felt more alive.

The inside of the Garage was stripped-down simplicity: painted black walls, the skeleton of lights stretched across the ceiling, a spinning mirror ball over the dance floor. Behind the DJ setup was a giant painted logo of a man holding a tambourine and covering his face with an oversized biceps, a "Paradise Garage" tattoo on it. On the dance floor was wall-to-wall Black and Brown, a community of the sweaty and blissful and ecstatic. Models and celebrities might've gone uptown to Studio 54, but the Garage was like the trenches. New York's beautiful and forgotten everymen and -women (and everything in between) plunged into this collective release. It was spiritual and tribal: the trancelike thumping beats mirrored our hearts, as though the music was playing from inside of us. Our veins pulsated to the rhythm, our bodies and our breaths moved in sync with the beat, with the world, with one another. You got so locked in that it felt like your dancing was creating the music and if you stopped it would all go silent.

People took dancing seriously there. The Garage even had dressing rooms where some people would change out of their dress clothes into their sweat clothes. Girls would come out in their cropped T-shirts and pum-pum shorts, coming to dance the way some people go to the gym. Our trio didn't go for that; we kept all our dress clothes on because they were part of the effect, selected specifically because of how they moved when we danced. People don't think much about the way clothes are a kinetic extension of the body, but we put a lot of stock in that.

Before we got there we would usually smoke reefer, sniff a little cocaine if we could get our hands on it. The Garage didn't sell alcohol—which is why it could stay open all night—but there was a free bowl of lemonade there that was spiked with mescaline. After a few hours on the dance floor, I lost all sense of time and separation between myself and the music. Behind my eyes flashed the memory of being a boy at Mr. Cotton's club with my dad, watching the adults flood in and come to life on that floor. It was like I was inside of the memory, watching myself watch myself.

The DJ booth was like an altar, and at the Garage the man behind the turntables—and the orchestrator of the whole scene—was Larry Levan. Larry was a visionary, an artist, and a pioneer of House music, turning what became called Garage House into its own genre. The sound system in there was renowned—you felt every beat and instrument through the floor—and Larry was a tastemaker. If the crowd wasn't feeling one of his choices, he'd play it over and over and over again until he won them over. And he always did. The music was both strange and familiar to me. House music grew out of the up-tempo R&B and soul I grew up on, so my own history was tied up with the music's. I intuitively understood it at a level beyond thought, beyond language.

Robin couldn't dance for shit—she had this white-girl thing she'd do with her arms—so I taught her how to move. We'd dance with Darlene at the Garage until morning, that electric thump coursing through our veins, the confetti drizzling down onto the crowd. They call it a groove because there's room for you to fit inside of it, and that space feels like it's been dug especially for you. Dance music is about repetition, and the more you do it, the more you are caught inside a ritual, doing something so long and so intensely that it begins to do you. At dawn, we'd watch the sun coming up through the open roof, the sky starting to turn a magical light blue, the sweat on our bodies like we'd been washed in religious exaltation.

Damn, if it didn't feel like we were going to live forever.

We hit all the clubs of that era: Better Days, Ariel's, Danceteria, the Door. No one cared how old I was, where I came from, what my mother thought, or who I was during the daytime. I never felt attractive—I didn't have the wavy hair, light eyes, or light skin that turned heads. I was this bucktoothed, dark-skinned boy, wearing all black, almost disappearing in those dark clubs, hoping someone would see me.

But the more I went, the more I found people like me—tired of hiding, wanting to be seen. That world exposed me to a different way of being, of living, an alternative to what I knew. I met a community of people who also didn't fit in their own homes and neighborhoods, so they came here, and together we joined up and formed our own.

The hood puts certain labels on you and has a certain understanding and limits on who and what you can be. Robin gave me a license to free myself: to want and be wanted, to dance and open up, to explore who I was in a way that Vanderveer would never allow. Robin invented an identity for me that I'd transform into when we crossed the East River into Manhattan. His name was Kenneth Banjee, and he was powerful and confident and desirable. There was nothing insecure about Kenneth, and though it started as something of a joke, seeing myself through Robin's eyes was transformative. You can't be something else if you can't even picture it. Robin saw it long before I did.

"D, what are we gonna do here about Kenneth?" Robin yelled to Darlene in the sleeping city dawn. "What we gonna do about this man?!"

The three of us were wandering down West Fourth Street. The sun was coming up behind the buildings, the puddles glistening, the strange orange light shimmying off the stone. Our plan that night was to sleep in the park, which we usually did. It was run-down and rat-infested but we'd crash together under a tree—always with the shades and hats tipped forward. In the morning, we'd wash our faces in the public bathrooms, get a pizza slice, and head back to the runway to do it all again.

That night we were still electric from hours of dancing, sweating in the cold air, coming down but still vibrating. We weren't going to let the night end on our watch.

"What we gonna do about Kenneth?" Robin was shouting to Darlene, but also to the world. "Is he gonna be a model? A dancer? New York, do you see this man? Kenneth, get over here, you sexy motherfucker!" she said, linking my arm. Darlene caught up and hooked into my other arm and we went looking for a spot to watch the sun rise.

One of our rituals was to find a scenic spot in the city—balconies, parks, piers—that we thought of as hidden. Places of aesthetic beauty. Places where the majestic city could reveal itself to us. Places we could call our own. Places where we could dream.

We'd sit there playing our little radio, smoking our own individual blunts—as the Rastas do—and drinking Babycham or Budweiser. We'd commune, laugh, talk about where we were going to end up, as though we could conjure our future into being. Darlene was going to live in the Madonna building in Park Slope, Robin on Fashion Avenue, and I was going to live in a high-rise building at the bottom of Fifth Avenue at the entrance to Washington Square Park.

When the drinks were empty and the blunts out, someone would say, "C'mon, guys, bring it in," and we'd huddle up to "christen the spot." We called it the Circle. We'd put our arms over each other's shoulders and press our bodies together: sometimes we'd cry, or scream, or just hum and moan, let out our pain, our love. Then we'd say, like a prayer: "*To each new day, we're gonna make a new day.*" At my lowest, I would always think back to that pact, of its promise, of the magic inside of it. Dancing in the clubs freed me but the Circle grounded me, gave me hope that maybe life could always be like that.

If that's all it ever was, I probably could've died happy. But those nights were just a slice. I still had to spend most of the week in Vanderveer, with my mother, with a school that wanted nothing to do with me, with dudes who walked all over me, with the trauma that wouldn't let me be, with the emptiness that showed up like clockwork once I came down.

Back home, hard drugs had started to scoop out the heart of the projects. At first, cocaine seemed like something glamorous. At the clubs I'd watch women in feather boas sniff it off thick glass tables through dollar bills and then dance all night. I didn't like putting things up my nose, and it was expensive, so I did little more than try it here and there.

I didn't even know you could smoke it until Robin showed me.

One morning before school, Robin called me and told me to come downstairs to her apartment. When I got there, she went into her father's room and dug out a big brown vitamin jar of powder cocaine from behind his headboard. She brought it into the kitchen and cooked it up on the stove, like she knew exactly how to do it. I sat on the living-room couch, half paying attention. "What you doing over there, girl?" I asked.

Robin put a single finger over her mouth, like *shhh*.

Then she brought out this purple chalice, a gorgeous pipe, and gave me the first hit. She watched me closely with those fierce blue-gray eyes as I inhaled.

"How do you feel?" she asked.

"It's cool," I said, coughing it out. "It's ai'ght."

"Kenneth, promise me one thing," she said. "Promise me that you'll never do this with anyone else except me."

"Yeah, Pook," I said, "no problem."

She was not playing. "No, listen," she said, dead serious. "I'm *not* fucking around. If I find out you're smoking this shit without me, I'm gonna kick your ass," she said. "For real." She could, and she meant it.

"Okay, okay. Damn. You got it," I said. "I won't. I promise."

I left her apartment and took the train to school, not feeling much beyond a nice, smooth feeling. It seemed easy enough to keep my promise. I couldn't imagine pulling off this elaborate science project on my own, so I didn't think much of it. But that morning, the seeds had been planted. I'd soon break that promise to Robin, and many others too. Over and over and over again.

The bell had been rung.

# CHAPTER 6

# STRUNG

*Those on the pipe are so coke-crazed,*
*so hungry for that ready rock that even*
*hardcore dope fiends are apt to show disgust.*
*A man can carry an addiction to heroin,*
*or at least he can pretend to carry it;*
*cocaine always carries the man.*

—David Simon and Ed Burns, The Corner

**NEW YORK CITY**
**1985**

"MICHAEL," MY MOTHER USED TO TELL ME, "WE'RE from a long line of drunks." She'd say it casually, like she was talking about what part of the Bahamas her family came from or the coarseness of our hair. Her generation didn't talk about addiction as a disease, though it ripped holes through her family just as sure as cancer. That tornado was gathering inside me too, hiding in my blood, waiting to unleash its damage. Addiction is my legacy as much as the darkness of my skin and the sound of my voice.

What most people don't realize about addiction is that it

is in you before the drug even shows up. That's because the drug itself is not the problem; it is a *symptom* of the problem. The drug is the culmination, the *final* step—not the first. The very first time I smoked cocaine in Robin's apartment, I was already an addict, I just didn't know it. I was a silent bomb waiting to go off, my brain looking for the right drug to take hold. And at eighteen, it found me.

During my last year of high school I ended up in an alternative GED program called CVC, City Volunteer Corps. It was a new program that Mayor Koch had just started where high school seniors worked in a service capacity for the city of New York for school credit. We painted the buildings of the Silver Lake Golf Course and the Staten Island Ferry terminal, planted trees in the parks, made and bagged all the ticker tape for the parade honoring Bishop Desmond Tutu's visit to the city. The first time I saw myself on television was when I was interviewed about delivering food to the elderly. The entire experience was good for me—far more influential than school was—and I felt part of something, like I mattered somehow. But as the months went on, I started to slide: sleeping late, skipping out, and sneaking off to sniff cocaine with my team leader.

At the end of our year, they offered graduates $2,500 in cash or a $5,000 scholarship to college. As far as I was concerned, there was no choice at all: I grabbed that money. Flush with cash, I was looking to go big with the celebration. The old standbys—reefer and beer—weren't going to cut it, not this time. I thought back to the year before, sitting on Robin's couch while she cooked up the cocaine for us. I had no idea how to do all that, but I knew you could get it in crystallized rocks, and ready to smoke.

*Ding.* Crack had found me.

I bought a vial on the Front Page—the intersection in front of Vanderveer—as easily as purchasing a carton of milk at the store. Then I broke a rock into little pieces and mixed it in with some weed in a blunt. Then the fire, the crackle, and the boom: a fireworks show drove through me like a truck. Like someone had lit a wick that ran through my body. From the warmth rushing in, the ringing in my ears, and the tingling of my joints, I was full-on electric.

Powder cocaine takes time to wind its way through your system, but smoking it in crack form is the express train. The dopamine and serotonin stream in, flood your bloodstream, and just wash away all your pain and doubts and inhibitions. What's left is a euphoria and diamond-sharp clarity, lucidity of speech and thought. Your body hardens in every way, making you invincible, unbreakable. And then, just when you're sure you can take on the world, it's gone. And all you crave is to get back to that tingle. It is literally all you can think about.

No one needs to tell you that crack is addictive. The drug's defining trait is how intensely you want more of it, how you'd do anything to get it. You go back for it again and again, chasing that original feeling, but you never get there. That's its nature—just enough to hook, never enough to satisfy. I smoked away most of my CVC money, sometimes with Darlene, often alone. A week, a month, a year vanished in a haze.

Once crack came into my life, it just moved the fuck in. Everything else took a backseat. At first it felt like this salvation, like I had filled a hole in me that I didn't think could be filled. None of that was true—I was really putting Band-Aids on gunshot wounds—but I bought into the lie because I needed to. The lie was so much more comfortable. You feel like the drug is brightening or enhancing your life. But then it becomes your life.

Drugs had long been a way I made myself matter. From the age of twelve, I was saving up my allowance to buy weed so I could roll joints and be part of the crowd. Having the reefer made me feel important, like I mattered to people. But with crack, it was like the opposite. The walls of my world closed tight around me, shutting out everyone and everything. I'd get high in stairwells, in alleys, on rooftops, anyplace where I could disappear. And that's exactly what happened: I disappeared.

"YOU OUT OF YOUR fucking mind, Kenneth?" Robin said, her face flushed and heated. "What in the fuck is wrong with you?"

When Robin found out, she came at me for real. This was no dainty girl; this was Robin, and she seemed ready to knock me out. I denied, deflected, made it like it was no big thing, but she wasn't having it. She had always acted like my protector, and that had meant protecting me from other people. But now it meant from myself. Robin had been convinced that I was going to become something, that I was going to take on the world. Now I was just another young Black man fading into the background, given in to the pipe.

"I can't believe you gonna fuck all this up," she said, but I wasn't hearing it. I had convinced myself that there was nothing for me *to* fuck up. Being an addict is about finding a reason to keep feeding your addiction—no matter what—so I convinced myself that I had to break free of Robin too. I told her to leave me alone and dodged her until she let me be. Anyone or anything getting in the way of my getting high was a problem. That's addiction in a nutshell right there.

Robin's absence brought Darlene and me closer together, with drugs acting as the glue. We were partners in this addictive spiral—on again/off again romantically—rebelling against the world, against Robin, against our parents. My mother still had her hands in everything I did, and Darlene's father was a Joe Jackson type who was trying to cultivate an Olympic career for her. Unlike me, Darlene had actually tasted what her gift could offer. She was already a track and basketball star when we met and could have had a future on that path.

I remember going with Darlene to a bodega to get some blunts and seeing the cover of the *Daily News,* with her picture in the lower-right corner. It was a story about the new women's basketball program in the city. I went wild, but she made it like it was no big thing. Darlene had already moved on in her mind. She told her father that she didn't want that life, that she was done with it. And I was there dropping out of my own life, so we caught each other on the way down. We were nineteen years old and completely strung out. No one knew the word "crackhead" back then, because our generation was the first. They invented the term to make sense of us, this new breed.

I avoided my mother as best as I could, but she could tell that something was off about me, far past normal. She convinced me to go to my first rehab: Samaritan Village in Jamaica, Queens. I went to a two-week orientation, where they processed me, gave me a physical, and detoxed me before they planned to send me upstate to the residential facility. On July Fourth weekend, a couple days before I was going to ride that bus north, I called my mother. "I wanna get out of here, Ma," I said, quietly into the phone. "Can I come home? I miss you."

"I miss you too, baby." I heard the breaking of her voice, the emptiness at the other end of the line. "Come home, baby."

"Okay," I said, pressed against the phone, a little boy aching for his mother. I just stayed on the line and cried with her. When I hung up, I splashed water on my face and got to packing up. Going out the front door would've meant too much confrontation; I was technically allowed to leave, but they wouldn't make it easy. So I opened up the second-floor window, tossed out my duffel bag, and jumped out after it. Hitting the ground with a thud, I went looking for a subway stop and took the train back home. Neither my mother nor I really understood what I was dealing with. The language of addiction and rehabilitation did not exist back then like it does now—not even in mainstream America, much less the hood.

When I relapsed around my twenty-first birthday, my

mother sent me to live with my father in Greeleyville, South Carolina, where he had grown up. He had a trailer house on old family property. My father's family were generations of farmers going back two hundred years before they owned the land, back to when *they* were owned along with the land. Years later, I learned that my father actually lived a few miles away from the rice and cotton plantation where his grand-parents were enslaved. At the time, I knew very little of that history though it coursed through me too, just like blood, just like the beast of addiction.

To his credit, my father tried. He would start these man-to-man conversations with me about my mother, try to explain his side of things, but I wasn't having any of it. Sure, my mother had thrown me out, but no way was I going to gang up with him against her. All I knew was the pain he left her with. "Don't you fucking talk about her!" I'd yell. "She's a saint!" I didn't have the maturity to see things from his side. His issues were valid too; she could be headstrong and emasculating and I knew that. I just wasn't yet in the place to forgive my father, or really understand him.

When the static became too much, I'd bounce around to other relatives down there. I was drinking and smoking reefer like crazy, but I didn't touch crack. When I'd finally had enough of the country life, I came back to New York City on a Greyhound bus and moved back in with my mother. She took me in reluctantly, maybe thinking if I lived there she could at least watch me. I got a temp job at a law firm and one day they sent me with some petty cash to run an errand. With that money burning a hole in my pocket, I got the itch and bought a vial in Washington Square Park and smoked crack for the rest of the afternoon. And I didn't go back.

"Get the fuck out," Mom said. "I just can't with you." My mother was at her wits' end and she didn't know what she was dealing with. We were both clueless about addiction and she was in the dark, doing what she thought made sense. She couldn't live with me anymore but she didn't want me on the street; she needed me nearby so she could watch me.

Her solution was to help me get a studio apartment across the street in another building in Vanderveer. She vouched for me with the management office and got it all set up, figuring it was time for me to be on my own, be a man, have my own place. Maybe giving me that independence and responsibility would motivate me, would help me get it together. But leaving an addict alone is just a surefire way for them to go deeper down the hole. All that apartment did was allow me to put up stronger walls around myself. I was already disappearing in my mind; now I was able to disappear for real.

"MIKE! YOU IN THERE? Open up."

I was dozing off when a knock came out of nowhere, broke the silence in my tiny world. I recognized the voice. *Dana.* A few years back, during the height of my time in the Village with Robin and Darlene, I met a tall and confident young woman from Newark. Dana was a few years younger than us and I'd see her from time to time around the clubs and we became party friends. She was always hustling out of there so she wouldn't miss the last bus to Jersey. I used to joke with her about how she must turn into a pumpkin at midnight.

I had disappeared from the scene for a while and was ditching phone calls, so Dana hunted me down in Brooklyn to check on me. She found me at that studio apartment and I opened the door. The second she saw my face, drawn and exhausted, she could tell that something had a hold of me. I told her the truth: crack had wiped me off the map.

"Well, you ain't doing that shit today," she said in her poised manner, stepping inside. "We're gonna drink some beer, smoke some weed, and just chill out." She had come to try to bring me back to myself with a case of Löwenbräu and some strong Afghani weed.

Later that night, nice and buzzed, we were lying around listening to Prince's *Sign o' the Times,* trying to hit those high notes on "Adore," laughing and talking. Dana was a private person and as the night went on, she began to open up a little more, confiding in me.

"Mike," she said, a secretive smile on her lips. "Listen, if I tell you something, you can't tell nobody."

"Sure, girl," I said. "What's up?"

"I'm about to get a record deal."

"Yeah, get it, girl," I said, lying on the floor near the speaker, passing her the blunt. "Be all you can be."

I didn't think she was serious. I figured it was a wish-fulfillment kind of thing, something she was putting out into the universe, like Robin and I used to do on rooftops. I knew dreams kept people going, so who was I to stomp on hers?

Visits like Dana's were rare, and that studio apartment

became both a hiding place and a drug den. My dealer, Bucky, was using it to cut and cook and stash his supply, tossing me some crack in exchange. If not for my mother, it's likely I would never have broken out of that world. But for a couple of weeks, my mother didn't hear from or see me. She had put me across the street to keep an eye on me, but I was locked in there, hiding from her, not answering her calls. My disappearance alarmed her. She sent people to check on me and I would look through the peephole and pretend I wasn't there.

Her anger boiled over to a point where she got the maintenance workers in the building to bust down my door. Then she threw me out, brought me back to her apartment, and handcuffed me to the bedpost.

Once I stopped screaming at her, I started to break down. "Ma," I said, my voice cracking, "just . . . just let me go." The words hung there between us. We both knew I didn't mean uncuff me; I meant let me *go*. Let me wither away.

She picked my face up in her hands, looked me in the eyes—serious as a heart attack—and said, "No."

That ferocity in my mother—the thing that caused me such pain—also saved my life. Her hardness meant I couldn't knock her down. No matter what I had become, she was never going to turn her back. It wasn't in her nature to do so. Thirty years earlier, she had pulled her own mother out of the jaws of addiction and now she was going to do it for her son.

It wasn't just Mom's toughness that saved me; it was her ties to the community. My mom had a network of connections in Brooklyn, including borough president Marty Markowitz, people at the tenants' association, and her close friend Marietta Smalls, who worked downtown for the city.

Mom knew what my weed smoking and drinking self was like, but this was something else. She knew I was on something harder, but she didn't have the tools to deal with a drug addict.

"Michael's acting crazy, Marietta," I heard my mom say on the phone in the kitchen. "I don't know what to do anymore."

"He's got to go away, Paula," she said. "He's got to go away for real."

Marietta knew about the crack epidemic that was whipping through the projects like a tornado, and she set my mom straight, explained what was going on. Marietta got me a bed at the only other place available at the time: Daytop Village Rehab.

Had my mother not had these relationships, I might have rotted away. All the mother's love in the world cannot save you without access to help, and during that time in Reagan's America, resources were snatched away from those who needed it most. Some of America got rich while a whole other America—Black and poor—was left to drown. Just getting a bed for me somewhere—anywhere—was something of a miracle.

PARKSVILLE, NEW YORK, 1988

Daytop Village was located in the Catskills of upstate New York, surrounded by tall green trees, open blue sky, and sloping mountains. It was another world from the cement and brick of Brooklyn, and on the bus ride up, as things took on those sharp colors, I couldn't even believe we were still in New York. Daytop was a former family resort decades past its heyday that had been converted into a drug rehab center. Red wood cabins with white trim, bunk beds with floral sheets, a cafeteria like in a public school, and a living room with a big fireplace.

As abnormal as the terrain was to me, the approach was even stranger. The counselors were looking for me to expose myself, literally the opposite of what I'd been doing since I was a kid. Opening up to others ran against everything I knew about how to survive in Vanderveer. DAYTOP is actually an acronym for "Drug Addicts Yield to Persuasion" and everything in that place was about pressing on you and seeing what came out. The programming was intense: various groups and sessions that broke down your negativity, analyzed your personality type, and re-engineered your habits and responses—not just to drugs but to everything. It's not something I took to naturally or right away, if at all. I had to learn to speak the language of addiction, foreign to a kid from the Brooklyn projects, like words from a lost civilization.

The feeling was mutual. I was like an extraterrestrial to the counselors there, who were used to dealing with heroin addicts, a group that carries a much different mindset from crack users. It's a generalization, but the addict's personality is an extension of the high itself. So heroin users are up and down; they get dopesick and rambunctious from the illness, but mostly they just chill or tune out. Crack smokers are some Machiavellian motherfuckers, sneaky and manipulative; we can run endless circles around former dope fiends, which is what these counselors were. I did my best to lie low and rarely spoke in group, but that was in direct conflict with the whole point of the program: shining a light on addicts so bright and fierce that it felt like open-heart surgery.

Our house manager was an old heroin addict named Walter, a big snarly dude whom I never saw smile. He walked around sipping his coffee, a cigarette dangling from his finger, running things with an iron fist. A turning point came around six months into my stay there. I was part of the Daytop Village Choir, which would go into New York City for performances and outings. After we came back from one trip, Walter invited us up to his office for a temperature check. He was debriefing everyone one by one, and then he got to me. "You're a newbie," he said to me, taking a sip of his coffee. "What did you think? Tell me about your trip." Before I could answer, his face clouded over, like he couldn't place me. "What's your name again?"

"Michael," I answered.

"And how long you been with us?" he asked, assuming I had just got there.

I knew what was coming. "About six months," I said, bracing as the words barely drifted out of my mouth.

His eyes went wide and he damn near spit his coffee out. "Six months!" The vein in his forehead popped and a storm gathered in his wide face. "You've been in my motherfucking house for six motherfucking months and I don't know your name!"

I tried to mumble something, but Walter stood up and started stomping around the office. "Six months, I'm supposed to know what you eat for breakfast every day! Where the fuck have you been hiding?" He got so upset that he had to go outside to cool down. I just sat there in fear.

They pulled me out of the choir, put me on punishment, and made me do chores like brushing the floor with a toothbrush. Walter instructed the counselors to ride me hard, past the point that I was willing to give. They took my privileges away and put a spotlight on me in the groups. After coasting for months, just getting by, that bright light made me so uneasy I wanted to get out of there. But they would give up on me before I ever did on them.

The three cardinal rules at Daytop were no drugs, no fighting, and no sex. Any one of these could be grounds for getting kicked out, but it wasn't about the act itself. Even having the *thoughts* was considered problematic; it was called "harboring ill." They trained us to get rid of these feelings by sharing our desires with someone else, a process known as "dropping your guilt." If you dropped your guilt on these thoughts and desires, you were all good. *Absolved.* That was the idea.

One evening, this overtly feminine guy in my group confided in me that he had feelings for someone else in the program. I listened supportively, encouraged him. "That's right," I told him. "Go on, drop your guilt," using the language I was trained to speak.

Soon after, he got busted for actually having sex with the person. When he was taken into a room and questioned, he said he'd dropped his guilt to me, which I hadn't revealed to a counselor. The counselors, already on top of me, figured I didn't say anything because I was planning on having sex with the same person. They held me in this room for hours, questioning me, rotating out interrogators, serving my meals in there until I would confess. "Cop to your guilt, son," they kept saying. "Admit that you wanted to have sex." I wouldn't break, because it wasn't true. But it read as intransigence.

"That's not true," I kept saying. "And I'm not gonna say it is. Not in this lifetime or the next."

When I wouldn't break, they threw me out. After thirteen months of intense treatment, I was dropped back into society without any services or reentry programming. The rehab process is supposed to take you from a place of extreme negativity to extreme positivity and then gradually help you find the balance between the two. Without a careful exit ramp, a reentry process, an addict is lost. I was raw and fragile, in no way ready to function back in society, sent back to Brooklyn like a premature baby dropped into the world.

# CHAPTER 7

# DAY ONE

**BROOKLYN**
**1989**

"HI, MY NAME IS MICHAEL, I'M AN ADDICT."

"Hi, Michael!"

Back in Brooklyn, I grabbed on to AA like a drowning man. I needed something to keep the momentum of rehab going, so I hit the meetings on Church Avenue in a small room on top of a storefront. It was a circle of foldout metal chairs on a scratched-up floor, stale coffee, and thick cigarette smoke hanging in the air like ghosts.

Even though I knew this was where I was supposed to be, I felt like the bastard child in there. The group was mostly older alcoholics who brought me in with one hand while pushing me away with the other. They said the right things but eyed me with suspicion, put me down, belittled my disease in a way they didn't do to each other. I wasn't expecting special treatment, but from the first moment in the door, I was given this black mark. More than once, I'd overhear them say something about "these fucking crackheads." It was never about me personally, but of course, it had to be. I was the crack addict in the room.

I got myself a sponsor, whom I'll call Bill—a tall, light-skinned family man in his thirties, proper and conservative. He had heart but also this militant toughness that didn't account for our differences. Bill's way of teaching was through putting me down, like he had seen it all and I was just some kid. Bottom line: he didn't think I could be trusted. It made everything about our relationship contentious.

For one, AA is built around how long you've gone since using—what "day" you're at—and the program does not recognize clean time in rehab. When I said I'd been clean for over a year, Bill said, "Un-uh. That don't count. That there was TC time."

"Tee what?" I asked.

"TC. Therapeutic community. You didn't have access to drugs; of course you're clean. Anybody can stay clean when they're locked in," he said, almost laughing at the idea. Others in the circle muttered in support. "Talk to me after you get three months in these streets," Bill said.

"Damn right," someone else weighed in, seconding the words like we were at church. I tried to protest, but they all shut me down. So my four hundred plus days of being clean—probably the hardest thing I'd ever done in my life—didn't mean a thing to them. I was back at day one.

A week or so after my first meeting, I mentioned something to the group about needing to get a job.

"A job?" one of them said, eyeing Bill.

Bill leaned forward, elbows on his knees. "You think you're ready for a job, son?"

I squirmed a bit in my metal chair. "Don't matter what I'm ready for," I said, "my mom ain't gonna let me—"

"How do you know that first dollar in your pocket won't take you right to the corner?" he asked.

When I didn't have a quick enough answer, Bill flashed me an *I told you so* look. "The program says you can't have a job for at least ninety days," Bill said.

"Ninety days?" I asked, my voice pitched high in surprise.

"At least," one of the other guys said.

"Ninety days until you can even *look* for a job," Bill said.

"You wanna try telling my mother that?" I said. She was already on me, how I was twenty-two years old and living under her roof. "Maybe that shit worked for you guys, but it's not gonna fly in my house."

"Those are the rules," Bill said. "Are you in the program or not?"

MY MOTHER WAS RELIEVED I wasn't dead, but she just didn't understand this new person I was trying to become, this new language I spoke. I was talking about working the twelve steps, dishing out all this therapeutic jargon, and brainwashed on extreme positivity. I was living the program but without the social skills needed to reacclimate to the world. It was like walking around with no skin—just my bare skeleton exposed—and everything that touched me hurt like hell.

She was on me all the time—about sleeping late, about eating her food, about not contributing. "Get off my phone!" my mom would yell. "Why you always on my phone? You don't pay for that. You're up in my house, grown man, and not helping out with shit."

"Ma, I need to confront you about the way you speak to me," I said calmly. "I don't like how that made me feel."

She made a face like I'd just spoken Greek. "What the hell are you talking about?" she said, exasperated. "How it made *you* feel?"

"I'm not Bunny, Ma. You can't just talk about me any way you want. I need to confront you about—"

"Confront me?" she asked, her eyes full of steam. "Who the hell you think you are, boy, confronting me? What the hell is wrong with you?"

In ways big and small, I was maturing, learning who I was, getting closer to the white meat, but my mother didn't want to know that person. We clashed as we always did, re-playing some old arguments like I was twelve years old again, like who was I hanging out with and why I couldn't be like my brother. But we also discovered some new ones.

Partly because of that pressure, I started to Scotch-tape something of a life together. During my time at Daytop, I had begun taking satellite courses in business management, and when I came home I rolled those over to Borough of Manhattan Community College (BMCC). As I watched the new generation of kids coming up at Vanderveer, I could see there was nothing going on. There was nowhere else to go, no talk of opportunities. Our horizons were right outside our door. I'd go to class, go to AA, and then get my look right and hang out on the block. My mom would ask where I was going, and I would make up some reason to go to the store, then buy a blunt, pack it with weed and smoke it, and head to the corner.

After around three months, I got a temp job at Pfizer Pharmaceuticals, working in the blueprint department in midtown Manhattan. My sponsor gave me a hard time about it, like I wasn't ready, like I didn't respect my sobriety. We'd argue about it all the time; I was trying to get my life together and the AA guys treated me like I was being an irresponsible kid, like I was just some crackhead who didn't know a damn thing.

I'd walk in there and Bill would beeline right for me. "How much money you got in your pocket? Did you smoke crack today?" Some of the other older dudes started talking like that too, condescending to me. I felt ostracized; they didn't know me and didn't try to know me. I was young and stubborn, sure, but I was lost and in pain and looking for some guidance. What I got instead was rules and judgment. I was a crack addict in a room full of alcoholics, and they didn't do anything but look down on me. So I stopped going to meetings.

The only person who was there for me for real was Robin. She never gave up on me, and when I got out of Daytop she came right to my door. We bonded all over again, hanging out and dancing, reaching for that brief flicker of youth. But there was something missing about it that I couldn't put my finger on. I still loved to dance, but the hope in those nights, the possibility, had drained out of them. We were older now.

The good times had led to some darkness and the two things could not be separated.

One night Robin and I ran into a group of people who used to hang with Dana, my Newark friend who had come to visit me when I was a crumbling shell in my studio apartment.

"Where's Dana at?" I asked. "I've been looking everywhere for that girl."

"You don't know?" one of them said.

"No, what?" I got a little nervous. Bad news usually came at the end of that question.

"Dana on the radio!" she said.

"No shit! Seriously?" I was stunned. This was about as likely as hearing Dana had moved to Venus.

"Yeah," she said, "she goes by Queen Latifah now."

"Queen La-what?"

"Latifah," they all said in unison.

"She got a record out!" another one said.

*Holy shit*, I thought. Dana was serious. To call it surreal would be an understatement. The percentage of people who break through in the arts is a tiny number, especially where I come from. It's a minuscule crack, and Dana had pushed herself through.

Every Friday DJ Marley Marl would have "The Hip Hop Mix" on the radio, WBLS. I'd lie on the floor of my mother's living room waiting for them to play Dana's record so I could record it onto my mixtape.

Dana hadn't just made it; she was a breakthrough—unabashedly feminist and politically conscious. She brought a voice to hip-hop that was brand-new, one that people responded to in droves. At the time, hip-hop was almost exclusively considered a man's game, and she played a huge part in changing that.

There's an old saying: A child can't aspire to be what he doesn't see. Dana had been a kid just like me, running around the same New York streets, talking about the same kind of outlandish dreams. Seeing her break through like that was a shock to the system. She made the whole thing tangible. I latched on to Dana—not hanging on her but just watching, studying her. I looked at her as a portal and, to her credit, she never denied me access. No matter how big she got, I always had her real phone number and she always made time for me.

So this was my world—taking classes, working a temp job, seeing Dana make her dream a reality—when Janet's "Rhythm Nation" exploded onto my mother's TV screen in September of 1989. When I danced along to that video, picturing myself alongside Janet, it was not a fantasy. It was about breaking free and realizing a dream; I just had to dig in to figure out how to manifest it.

I was still sleeping in my childhood bedroom, eating at the same kitchen table, still hanging in the courtyard—it was like my life had gone back to the beginning. A new decade was about to start, and I was still stuck in the same old place. After a year at Pfizer I was given three raises and a permanent position in the company headquarters on Forty-Second Street, a towering black and glass building near the Chrysler Building. The job wasn't exciting, but it paid me well enough that I could start saving up.

Around this time I ran into an old friend of mine, Victor,

who invited me to a housewarming party in Queens. While there I met his business partner, Kevin, whom I clicked with almost immediately. Kevin was a model and aspiring dancer, and the two of them told me about the finishing school that they were running in West Harlem. It was enticing to hook up with people who had some things going on. They told me about a friend of theirs who was renting rooms in the Bronx in one of those old prewar buildings with the high ceilings. I took one of the rooms and started to hang around Victor and Kevin, a little aimless, figuring out how to live on my own.

Early on, I tagged along with Kevin to a rehearsal for a fashion show he was putting on. Kevin was a handsome guy with dark skin, hazel-brown eyes, and perfect, gleaming white teeth. He had a permanent twinkle in the eye, always smiling and bubbly. Anything he said had this low undercurrent of laughter beneath it. But when Kevin walked out onto the floor to address the group of models, he transformed.

"All right, everybody, let me get your attention!" he barked, like a man who'd never not been in charge. He just became someone else, right there in front of my eyes. It felt supernatural, the way he turned it on. It was the first time I'd ever seen a person *become* someone else in front of me, and it astounded me: it seemed like a magic trick.

When he was done talking to the group, Kevin approached the woman in charge: "How we doing for Saturday?"

"That boy you brought in vanished on me, Kevin," she said. "Now I'm one short."

"You need someone to fill in?"

"One more male model," she said.

I was just sitting there twiddling my thumbs, waiting on Kevin. He turned to me. "Mike? What do you think?"

"Can you model?" the woman asked, a little impatient.

"What? Oh no, sorry," I said politely, clueless. "I don't model."

"He's in," Kevin said to the woman. "He'll be here tomorrow."

I mumbled something like "thanks" before Kevin escorted me outside.

When we got out the door, Kevin taught me my first show-business lesson. "You wanna be in this business, Mike? If someone asks you if you can do something, the answer is always yes. *Always*. Don't matter if it's fucking juggling or break dancing. You say yes and then you figure that shit out later."

Lesson learned.

I faked my way through a few rehearsals, learned the basics of how to walk and stand and turn. After that, Kevin and Victor invited me to join their finishing school. Every Saturday I would walk across the Harlem River Bridge to Amsterdam Avenue to go to class, which was in the basement of Kevin's father's toy store. There were classes on modeling, fashion, and etiquette. Kevin and Victor's ultimate goal was to lure in clientele and turn the school into a modeling agency.

After the course was done, we sold tickets for a modeling competition, which I invited my mom and some other family to. I remember watching from the wings as they all got up in the middle of the show and walked out. It wasn't for her, she told me later, shuddering as if I had done something unseemly. It cut deep—I felt like I was getting somewhere, doing *something,* and my mom turned her back on me. But her disapproval just made me lean into it harder.

I quit my job at Pfizer and dropped out of school, both of which were getting in the way of auditions and gigs I was trying to book. The arts is not a nine-to-five world and I felt like if I was in, I had to go all in. My mother thought it was a boneheaded move. This wasn't just messing around as a kid; this was throwing away a good job and a degree to chase some silly dream. But I knew I had to commit. I couldn't reach the next trapeze unless I let go of the first one. I had to step out into the void before the bridge would appear.

I think I had the right idea, but unfortunately, I fell flat. The modeling gigs didn't come consistently and then mostly dried up. I lost my ability to pay rent, got kicked out of my apartment, and bounced around different couches in Brooklyn. During that time I got back in touch with an old friend of mine, a talented music producer and songwriter named Anthony. Anthony was working with a few R&B groups that had already broken through. Anthony invited me to come and hang out on-set for a music video he was working on. When I got there, I felt this magical energy in my bones, being so close to something I wanted to do. But when I saw Anthony, he looked like a different person, much skinnier with hollow eyes. His face was also covered in makeup and he wasn't in the video, so I wondered why. I turned to a mutual friend. "Hey, why is Anthony wearing all that makeup?"

"Oh," she said, her voice dropping to a whisper. "That's to hide the lesions."

I didn't even know. He hadn't said a word. Anthony didn't have much time left—he had full-blown AIDS, and he succumbed soon after, right before the world was about to know his name. At a get-together with friends to honor his passing, I threw away my sobriety. And once the seal was cracked, it got much easier. I would get drunk on benders regularly. The voice in my head always rationalized that since I wasn't smoking crack, I was fine. But it's a slippery slope. After a series of blackouts, I landed back at home with my mother. Within an hour of walking in the door, she was harping on me to get a job if I wanted to stay there. Just to get her off my back, I started working at the Gap in Midtown.

Around this time I got my first dancing "gig." Heather Hunter, a former adult star who was branching out into music, contacted me through a mutual friend. She had a gig at Sound Factory Bar and her dancers had backed out at the last minute. She asked if I would dance up onstage with her. At my favorite club, doing what I love to do—with no one in my way—getting paid for it? Oh hell yes.

One day while I was working at the Gap, a handsome Latino guy in his early twenties walked in with his girlfriend. A voice in my head told me to walk up to him and engage him. I was moving around on the scene, in the clubs, trying to meet people. And there was something about him that made me approach him.

"Hey," I said, laying it on a little thick. "You look so familiar. Are you a dancer?"

His ego just glommed onto that. It turned out his name was Chad, and *why, yes, he was a dancer*. We got to talking.

"You dance?" he asked me.

"Just in the clubs," I said, "but that's my dream. I want to be a dancer so badly."

"Okay, well, maybe I got something for you," he said. "Take my beeper number. Give me a call."

Chad was working as a choreographer and had a slate of dancers whom he got gigs for. Once he saw I was for real, he hired me as a stand-in, like an understudy. "I'm going to train you and keep you on standby in case I ever need a dancer," he said. "If one of my dancers ever falls sick, you'll fill in, but I gotta clue you in to the choreography."

Chad and I would meet up at Broadway Dance Center on West Forty-Fifth Street. In between their official ballet and jazz classes, we would sneak in and use one of the rooms to practice, then run back out before the teacher came back in. In those fifteen-minute blocks, Chad taught me all his choreography. When we got busted, the school invited us to come in on the scholarship program: he had to clean the bathrooms and I did the punch cards downstairs in exchange for the right to use the space.

Chad brought me into his stable of dancers, a young and vibrant group that I latched on to like a wide-eyed kid. The dance world was a tight community, competitive but supportive, and it ran like a connective tissue through all points of the city. People working service jobs, going to school, putting in late and weekend hours to make it—all connected by this passionate, invisible force. Dancing requires connection; it is about communicating with one voice, operating in unison. I loved the power of it: how a group of strangers can go into a room and then come out as one. I felt I had been alone for so long and dance was the thing that tethered me to others. There was this desire in me to study every nook and cranny of the craft; I'd never had that feeling before. I wanted to take it in and release it out of me as naturally as my breath.

Hooking myself into this group of Black and Brown artists practicing, networking, and auditioning felt hopeful and open and filled with possibility. It was an echo of those first nights out in the clubs with Robin. I spent any hour I could at 440 Lafayette, an iconic rehearsal studio and audition space in the Village, which was like the hub of that scene. Polished hardwood floors and ballet barres, mirrored walls, and some of the most talented dancers in the world.

I still got the occasional modeling gig, which was mostly just to get out there and make a little money. And I knew the modeling and dance worlds were adjacent. In the summer of 1991, I was twenty-four and had just booked a major campaign as spokesmodel for a company, Rock Embassy, who made official touring jackets for the likes of Janet Jackson, Public Enemy, and Madonna that sold at the concerts. I felt like I was on the verge of something, anticipating some kind of break, excited to start seeing my face out there.

Sometime that summer, I was cutting through a courtyard at Vanderveer, on my way to the subway to go to a dance rehearsal in Manhattan, when someone grabbed me from behind. I was thrown against the fence, and I felt a gun pressed hard to the side of my head. The pressure of the metal on bone sent a shock through my body. The voice in my ear, high-pitched and screechy, like Eazy-E. "Where's it at? Where's it at?" Hands were patting at my jacket, at my pockets, at my pants.

"Yo, I—I don't got anything," I said, my voice barely eking out.

"Naw, naw. It's not him," another, deeper voice said. "It's not him. Wrong dude."

And just like that the two guys walked off in the other direction. I never even turned around, didn't look at them. I kept on my way, walking toward the train, telling myself to shake it off. But my body wouldn't let me and my legs were straight-up *wobbling*.

I was lucky to escape that confrontation, but soon after, another one would show up. And instead of walking away, I ran full-speed right into it.

# CHAPTER 8

# SCARS

SOMETIMES, WHEN I CATCH A GLIMPSE OF MYSELF in the mirror, it still catches me by surprise. Just for a second. Then I remember. How easily it could have not happened. How the slightest change of plans, or a different decision in the moment, and I would be someone else. But we are the sum total of our choices, and I can't escape that truth. It's written right down the middle of my face.

The night that would change my life began with me being too exhausted to move. That week I was in rehearsals for a dancing job with Izora Armstead, one half of the Weather Girls of "It's Raining Men" fame. We were scheduled to leave for London the next week. The night of November 21, a Thursday, was the eve of my twenty-fifth birthday. After getting home to my mom's after practice, I collapsed on my bed, wiped beyond recognition, when a high school friend, E, called.

"Hey, let me take you out for your birthday," he said. "Come into the city and let's grab a drink."

"Nah, man," I said. "I'm wiped the fuck out."

"C'mon, Mike, just one drink. We gotta celebrate."

Gravity was doing its thing, not letting me move, much less go out into the night. Dancing can be hell on your body, even a young body. Your calves burn, your feet get heavy, your hamstrings are jelly. "Nah, my friend's throwing me a big party tomorrow," I said. "Come to that. I don't want to take the train back into Manhattan and—"

Then the rustle of the phone being picked up in the other room. "Michael!" It was my mother.

"I'm on the phone, Ma," I said. She'd heard it ring; she knew what she was doing.

"Michael, get off my phone, boy."

"Okay, one second!" I yelled, embarrassed, livid. I was twelve years old all over again.

E didn't say a word, but there was this thing hanging in the air: *Your moms still do you like that? Damn.*

"You know what," I said. "Fuck it. Where you wanna meet up?"

I put on a jacket from the Rock Embassy campaign, which had come out that week. It was for Madonna's Blond Ambition Tour, and I flipped it so the orange lining was on the outside, put on a pair of Doc Martens, tucked my jeans into my boots, and took the subway out to Manhattan. I hooked up with E and his friend, who later that night drove us out to Queens. Around midnight we were at a small bar on Jamaica Avenue and I was pretty hammered, drinking what I called "the potion," Bailey's and Absolut.

There was a small dance floor in there and I was showing off a bit. When a pro is on the floor, there's a little circle that tends to happen, with people stopping and watching. After getting up a good sweat, I needed a break, telling E, "Yo, I'm a go outside and get some air."

Out on the sidewalk, I saw a group circled around a dude I knew from Brooklyn named Jamaican John. There were three or four of them, all up in his face. John seemed relaxed, in control, but the alcohol had lit something in me. The embarrassment from my mother still lingering, hovering over me like a cloud, got me acting stupid. "Fuck that, John!" I said, calling out. "Ain't nobody jumping you out here. I got yo back, bro. The ni**as inside are from Brooklyn and we all gonna wild out!"

"Mike," John said, calmly, "mind your business and go inside. I got this." His tone told me I was making it worse, and his eyes said *get lost*. So I went back into the bar.

I might've had another drink. But soon after, the night had done its thing where it reached its collapsing point; everything had already peaked. When I found E, I told him to grab his friend, who was driving us, so we could bolt.

"All right," E said, "let me tell him we want to head out."

"Okay," I said. "I'll be outside waiting for you."

When I went back out front, that group of dudes hassling John had broken up, but one of the guys was still out there. He was slim, dark-skinned, in his twenties, a basic approximation of me. He approached me, gave me a look up and down, and then started pacing behind me.

"What's your problem, bro?" I said. He was silent, but he stayed behind me. "What you keep walking by me for?" I could feel him in back of me, sizing me up, making this squelching, teeth-sucking sound. I got a little nervous, but I kept that in.

"C'mon, man," I said, "fuck all this shit, we all brothers out here. We all Black! What we out here like this for?"

"What? What?" he said, leaning in. Then he kept repeating that over and over. "What?" The pacing, the sucking, the "What?"—like in a hypnotic loop. Then he stepped in front of me and we were face-to-face. In a flash, he swiped his hand across his mouth and smacked me right across the face with what felt like an open hand.

I was more surprised by it than anything. *That's all you got?* I thought. *You smack dudes?* I charged at him and we got into it on the sidewalk. Then his crew jumped in and started whaling on me, one with a metal bar of some kind. I was rolling around until someone dragged me out from under them. It was E, and once I got to my feet, the two of us ran halfway down Jamaica Avenue. When we stopped, hands on our knees, catching our breaths, I caught sight of E's arm: he had blood squirting out of his wrist like a whale's head. I took off my shirt and wrapped it around his wrist like a tourniquet.

"Thanks, man," he said. When he looked up and saw me, the color just drained out of his face. "Mike, it's cool," he said, pushing down the panic. "It's cool. You—you're gonna be all right. It's okay."

"What?" I asked. "What are you talking about?"

"You gotta a little—a little touch in the face," E said, gesturing to his own face. I put my hand to my cheek and forehead and felt the wetness there. It was an unseasonably warm night, so I first thought I had been sweating. But then I saw the dark liquid on my fingers. Under a streetlight, in a parked car's side mirror, I saw it: this gigantic cavern of blood rushing down the middle of my face. The guy hadn't been slapping me. He had been cutting me open.

In prison, guys learn to hide razors in their mouths so they can quickly grab them and cut someone; it's called "spitting a razor." That teeth-sucking sound was him getting the razor ready between his teeth; he had swiped it down my face, from my forehead, across the bridge of my nose, down my right cheek almost to my jawbone. He must have cut me a second time on the ground, because there was a stream of blood rushing down the left side of my neck too. It had all happened so quick and the adrenaline was flowing so fierce that I hadn't even noticed. The blood continued to gush out of me like a flood. In a mix of anger and panic, I just saw all red. Ready to kill him, I ran back up the street.

It was chaotic in front of the bar. One of E's friends had been beaten nearly unconscious and E was losing so much blood that he seemed like he was going to pass out. Our friend pulled up in his Pathfinder and just said "Get in" to all of us. We all piled in and he drove us down the street to Jamaica Hospital.

IN THE EMERGENCY ROOM, it all gets blurry. I was in and out—still pretty drunk, likely in some shock. The pain was excruciating, a tearing in my skin, a burning like someone had poured gasoline on my face and then lit a match. One of the nurses told me that the cut down the side of my neck was just inches from my jugular, which would've killed me right there on the sidewalk. "You should feel lucky," she said.

That's about the last thing I felt.

Throughout the night and into the next morning, ER doctors would come in to try to stitch me up and I'd have to fight them off. "You can't stitch me up!" I yelled. "I need a plastic surgeon. I'm a model and you'll ruin my career if you stitch me up." The nurses would pour saline solution on my face to prevent infection, which burned even worse, like my skull was on fire.

When the police came in, I told them I was the victim of a violent attack. In the haze, I'd remembered hearing about a model a few years back whose face got cut up by a stranger and she had to depend on other people to give her money for the plastic surgeon. Since then the city made victims of violent crimes eligible for the medical insurance that would pay for one. Otherwise, there's no way on earth I could've afforded it. If the ER had stitched me up, I would've looked like a Batman villain, the front of my face marked up like train tracks.

By the next morning, when the plastic surgeon came in, I couldn't see at all out of my right eye. The skin underneath had been exposed to the air so long that it had rolled back like a canvas, literally covering that eye. When the procedure started, they had to strap me down in the gurney and hold my head in place. I wasn't put under and I don't remember any anesthesia; what I do remember is that I felt everything. It was a pain so excruciating that I didn't wish it on my worst enemies.

When it was over, I didn't have the courage or strength to

ask for a mirror. Days went by before I saw what I looked like.

I went home to my mother; it was Thanksgiving week, so we had family there, aunts and cousins. When I walked into the house and she saw my face, she just lost it.

"I'm so tired of this," my mother said. "Why do you keep doing this to me?"

"To you? I just had my face cut open!" I yelled. "What the fuck, Ma?"

"You trying to kill me, son? Is that it, are you trying to—"

"What the fuck? How about asking me if I'm okay?"

"Don't you dare talk to me like that, come in here all cut up and telling me—"

"That's fucked-up, Ma. How can you be so—"

She walked out of the room and yelled back to me through the walls. "You know what? I'm gonna take out an extra life insurance on you. You are not going to leave me stuck with the bill for burying you. You're not going to live to see thirty. I can see that now."

I turned around and walked right out. I hid, went underground. For a few months I was homeless, sleeping in spare rooms, on couches, on floors, staying with whoever would take me in. Darlene had an apartment in the Queensbridge projects and I stayed with her for a while. I had to leave the dance job with Izora, the one that would've taken me to London. There wasn't enough time for my face to heal.

In a sick twist of cosmic fate, the Rock Embassy ad campaign came out that week and my face was in magazines, on subway walls, on billboards, all over the city—the smooth face that I would never have again. It was surreal. Everywhere I looked was my face—I'd finally made it—but it was no longer my face. It was someone else up there.

When I looked in the mirror, it was this other person. This deformed stranger. A face that I didn't even want to look at.

The cut healed into one big swollen line and I never felt more ugly, more hideous. I was ashamed. I got stared at. I couldn't wash my face, so I started to break out. After they took out the stitches, I had to keep the scar protected with greasy ointment. I felt like I had to hide: under ballcaps pulled low and hoods turned up and anything that would help blend me into the background. As the cut healed, it was a thinner line, neater, but it was still swollen, raised on top of my skin. No matter how much I felt like disappearing into the crowds, it started to feel like eyes were always on me.

I tried not to feel sorry for myself—everyone out there was hustling, trying to get something going. I assumed that was a wrap for my modeling career but that as a dancer I'd be fine. People don't stare at dancers' faces. My dancer brothers and sisters embraced me tighter, told me they loved me and, more important, let me feel it. They showed up for me. I was teetering on some serious depression at the time and the arts rescued me. That's why I say the arts saved my life: I mean it literally.

I remember around this time, running late for a dance audition, fixing my hair in the mirror. I used to love my hair: my flat top, my high top. That day I couldn't get the fade line to be even, so I kept moving the razor higher and higher. The next thing I knew I had no sides, just a plateau across the top of my head. I got really angry and then said "fuck it" and took the razor and went bald. It felt like a declaration. I heard the singer Seal say that people asked if his facial scars were "tribal markings," so I went down that route. I told people I had done some ancestry research, and I was in the same African tribe as Seal.

For the rest of my life I would have a five-inch scar across my face to make sure I never forgot what could have been. A gang sign on my face, what they call a buck-fifty. Me— *Faggot Mike*—the softest kid in the Vanderveer projects. Looking hard as fuck.

There was a lingering trauma to the attack that I never addressed, so it stayed with me. In restaurants, I refused to turn my back to the door, I'd look for the exits first thing when I entered a building. I was prescribed therapy and went once or twice but decided I didn't want to feel that. It was something else we don't do in my community. We don't talk about what we're feeling. *I'm just going to pull my baseball cap low and power through.* It was all about hiding. I shut it down, not knowing that those things will always find their way to bubble up. It would be years before I let myself feel the trauma of what happened.

I have another scar down my neck near my jugular that people don't notice, which I often grow a beard to cover; that's the one that could've killed me. Each year in the United States, three thousand men of color are murdered before their twenty-fifth birthday. I was an inch away from being a statistic. It's hard to feel worthy of being saved and, I admit, part of my motivation in giving back is the guilt from still being here.

The hood is no meritocracy; there was nothing special

about me that saved my life. It just wasn't my time. And as a reminder, that it all could be taken away, that it all could have gone differently, the scars. I can't look at my face without seeing them, and I've made peace with it. I've come to realize that this is as it should be. The scars are there, will always be there, like a message from the past, a repeating, haunting refrain in that voice I know so well: *Told you, son. Didn't I tell you? You see what you get?*

# CHAPTER 9

# THE BREAKS

*Everyone has art in them. It is our expressive language. The art expression is godly.*

—*Chuck D*

THE WINTER AFTER MY FACE GOT CUT, I WAS CRASH-ing all over the city, couches and spare rooms, wandering through some dark nights of the soul. In February, I was staying at a friend's apartment, a favor that had turned into an uncomfortable situation. It reached a point where he directly asked me to leave, but I had nowhere to go. That evening I was calling around, trying to figure out where to lay my head, when he got an incoming call. After answering it, he handed me the phone and walked off without saying a word.

On the phone was a breathless voice. "Man, I've been trying to track you down." It was Chad, my dancer friend and mentor. "Your moms told me where you were at."

"Hey, man," I said. "I can't really talk, I gotta—"

"Good news, kiddo," he said, talking right over me. "You're up. One of my dancers backed out."

"Wait, what?" I couldn't even process what he was saying. I had been thinking about basic needs like my next meal and where to sleep that night.

"I mean *pack your shit*," he said. "You're going to L.A. I have a gig for you with Kym Sims. You're flying out there in the morning. Joining their tour starting *to-morrow*," saying that last word with a dramatic flourish.

Kym Sims was a dance/pop star out of Chicago, where house music was born. She was working with the hottest producers, like Steve "Silk" Hurley and Maurice Joshua, and had a number-one hit with "Too Blind to See It," which crossed over from the clubs to the radio. Chad had gotten me on as a standby dancer for her tour, so I already had those routines down. All I'd needed was a lucky break to get me that last bit of the way to the stage. It didn't always happen, so the excitement hit me like shock. I knew decades, lifetimes, were sometimes spent waiting for that call.

"Holy shit," I said, my heart pushing through my chest. "Holy *shit*. Okay, I'll be there."

Chad started laughing. "No shit you'll be there. Told you I'd take care of you. Don't fuck this up, Mike." When he hung up, I was sitting there holding the phone, just about stunned speechless.

A giant wave washed over me, and I saw everything anew. Minutes earlier my world was low-ceilinged, cramped, and crowded. And with that call, it all opened up; light shone in, the world beamed expansive and endless. I started to pick up clothes and pack up my duffel bag in the living room, adrenaline coursing through my body and nowhere to channel it.

On the television that night happened to be the premiere

of Michael Jackson's new video, "Remember the Time." It's hard to believe now, but a video premiere back then was actually a really big deal. And a new Michael Jackson video? That was an all-out event, like, we're talking prime-time broadcast television, simultaneous channels, the whole bit.

Directed by *Boyz n the Hood*'s John Singleton, "Remember the Time" was a wildly expensive nine-minute video—a short film, they were calling it—with Eddie Murphy, Iman, and Magic Johnson in an ancient Egyptian palace. A series of performers try to entertain Murphy's pharaoh, while his bored wife, Iman, looks on unimpressed. Then Michael shows up, in his inimitable fashion, to blow their minds.

About six minutes in, there's the breakdown, when the song goes a cappella and the background dancers move in to join Michael. They pop in from behind the stone columns, limbs sliding in and out and back in precise rhythm, a take-off on the classic Egyptian-style moves. Their arms out, shoulders popping, feet sliding across the marble floor, that perfect Michael mix of rigid and fluid.

I was caught up in the absurd video, the contagious rhythm, drawn to Michael in his gold satin turtleneck and winged metal breastplate(!), when my eyes began to take in the faces of the other dancers. And my jaw must've dropped down to my feet. I couldn't believe it: *I knew these people.* These were New York dancers I had met, hung out with at 440 Lafayette, practiced alongside of. There was Big Lez. Josie. Stretch. And Link!

*Holy shit.*

It was surreal, like they had materialized there on the screen. Like they had reached through to the other side and manifested themselves there. Since I'd been a child, the TV had always been a portal to this other world, an unreachable space. But there they were. Then it hit me: *And I was going to be one of them.*

Just a couple of years earlier, I was dancing to Janet Jackson in front of my mom's television. Now I was watching her brother, dancing with people I knew, whom I'd worked with. I couldn't even wrap my head around it. *It's gonna happen. I'm gonna dance with Janet Jackson.* My eyes flooded with tears at the poetic beauty of it, the cosmic circle. I hadn't had a lot of moments where the world opened up like that for me, and I marveled at it, tried to breathe it all in while I had the chance.

BESIDES A COUPLE OF trips with my mother back to the Bahamas, I'd never been anywhere. Now I was getting out of Brooklyn. Not for a gig, a hustle, or even just a job. A *career.* The word felt foreign on my tongue. It was not something a lot of people talked about in East Flatbush.

In a blink, I was off: FedExed plane tickets, this city, that stadium, this hotel, that nightclub, going all over the country. I felt like a rock star. The Kym Sims tour led to more tours, for Technotronic, Ginuwine, Maya, and Crystal Waters, who made me her dance captain and would put me in her video for "100% Pure Love," which I also choreographed. (In the scenes of the three guys dancing in suits, I'm the skinny one in the middle.)

Performing onstage, for crowds, in stadiums, it's all about the energy you're receiving and then reflecting back. It's an electric relationship. They're taking you in and you're taking them somewhere. I was young and cocky, carrying a competitive edge up there. I wanted all eyes on me. I was a background dancer, but I'd act like those venues were filled up to see *me*. You couldn't convince me I wasn't Michael Jackson himself up there.

I saw some of the world—Italy, Germany, Austria, Japan—traveling with other dancers, and got a sense of where I fit in. I noticed how different my life had been from theirs. Most didn't come from drug-inflected backgrounds, were not exposed to the poverty or violence I was. They came from a world of performance arts schools and two-parent households and private lessons. I knew my mother wasn't rich, but I was in my late twenties before I understood how poor we were. Poverty doesn't feel like poverty when it's all you know, when you're surrounded by those just like you, when you can't conceive of any other way.

Breaking into that dance community was the first time I felt the difference between our worlds so profoundly. I didn't have the proper training, didn't know how to take care of my body, couldn't do a split, didn't know all the French dance terms. It motivated me, like: *It's showtime; you motherfuckers are going to gag. You are going to know I was here.*

I got a little cocky, arrogant, ungracious even. Dance had long come from a place of joy inside me, but when I first busted through, I carried this undercurrent of anger. I was striking back, dancing as confrontation, as assault even. I had never been allowed to fight, so I put that rage, that *violence*, into dance. That was how I saw it: *All you people who called me out, doubted me, picked on me, I'm gonna bust you open.* I didn't want just to be there; I wanted to stand out.

I remember once practicing my dance routine on a sidewalk, with my headphones and Walkman, and a lady on the street came up to me. "What is that you're doing?" she asked. "Is that martial arts?" I smiled; she wasn't that far off.

As the money began to roll in for the first time in my life, I treated it like my own plaything. I was young and immature, financially illiterate, selfishly not helping my mother out the way I should have. There was resentment toward her because she hadn't supported me, had never believed I'd make it. In fact, she had been this force I was battling, livid that I quit school and my job.

On tours I gravitated toward those few dancers who grew up like me, those with rocky pasts, because I wanted that connection, that synergy. It's not like we ever talked openly about poverty, addiction, or abuse. It was all locked up—we'd all learned the same rules about silence—but the connection was there, in the air. You'd catch subtle references or just see it in their eyes. You knew they knew and there didn't need to be a word said about it.

I found that bond with one of Crystal's other dancers, Kevin, a gay Dominican from the Bronx who didn't play around. He was short and muscular with dark-brown skin and bleach-blond hair. A catty dude who had a habit of sucking on his thumb, Kevin was funny and flamboyant, but down to whoop your ass if you disrespected him. He showed me that you didn't have to be one thing. He was gay, sure, and also the toughest motherfucker I knew.

I can now see how I picked up friends like shields. I sought out those I felt safe around—people like Robin and Kevin, the protectors that my dad and brother never were.

Those friends were like security blankets, and I latched on to them in case things went sideways, as I knew they could, as I suspected they would. I carried a fear that they were always just about to.

As my dancing career began to take off, the strangest thing started to happen. The scar down the middle of my face, the thing that made me want to hide, started to get me noticed. Not as a monster, like I felt, but as an object of curiosity, fascination, even beauty. Strangers would stop me on the street and say they found my scars striking and ask if they could photograph me. The first one I took up on this offer was a photographer named James Minchin III, whom I met while walking around Greenwich Village. He just walked up to me and said, "Hey, I'd love to photograph you, test shoot you. You got a good look." Later, I was hanging out with James in a dark room when the famous photographer David LaChapelle walked in. He stopped in his tracks and looked at me. "Oh my God," he said, "I want to photograph you."

It never occurred to me that anyone would want to look at me again, much less take my picture. It was literally the opposite of what I thought would happen. I tried to be gracious about this bizarre turn of events, seeing it as helping someone else's creative process, giving into this larger pool that we all put into. Directors started to see it too, so I began to get gigs in music videos, not even to dance. I guess the scar gave me a "look," or an "edge." It made me look like the tough guy I wasn't, but I was happy to pretend. That's all it felt like at first—pretending. *Sure, why not?* I've had so many people stop me and ask about the scar on my face that I think there's something else at work. I think the scar speaks to people's brokenness. We are all broken. And people found it astonishing, to see the inside made so visible. To see it marked in the flesh like that.

One of the first music videos I appeared in was for a Taylor Dayne ballad called "Send Me a Lover." I was holding a piece of white lace up to my face and the director, Randee St. Nicholas, explained that my character was in a broken romance, thinking of his lost love. So I rubbed this piece of lace across my face—in my mind, it was her panties—to remember the smell of her perfume. As they were shooting me, I got emotional, thinking about those I'd loved, lost, and hurt. It took me by surprise, like an ambush, this feeling like I wanted to cry. My defenses shot up and that voice appeared: *Don't you dare cry, Michael. Randee didn't tell you to cry. Fight the tears. Be a man, Michael.*

I was holding it in, forcing myself to make it through the shot, when Randee yelled cut.

"Whew," I said. "Thanks, Randee."

"Why?"

I smiled. "Well, to be honest, one more second and I wouldn't have been able to hold back the tears. I was going to full-on start crying."

Randee froze, her eyes big and bug-eyed. "What?! Why did you not cry?! Michael!"

"Wait, that would've been cool?"

I was the greenest dude on the planet, trying to give the director only what she wanted, nothing more. But I was also working against long-formed habits. I was conditioned in a world of the macho code, where being vulnerable put you at risk. Holding back the tears was an instinctual thing that men just learn to do, like breathing. But I'd find that most directors wanted to see that pain, even demanded it.

"EMOTE, MICHAEL! GIVE ME pain! Emote!"

The next year, I was at a shoot for a George Michael video and the director, Marcus Nispel, a tall German guy with a long bushy beard, kept screaming at me in his thick accent. The camera was right up in my face, my shirt was off, all these people and bright lights were around, and this guy was yelling at me full-bore.

"Emote, Michael!" he was yelling in a thickly accented growl. "Emote!"

*Emote? What the fuck does "emote" mean?* I didn't even know the word but was too embarrassed to admit it.

"Give me pain, Michael," he yelled at me. "Give me pain!"

That I understood. So I started to fake it, and then . . . something happened. It awakened something in me. In order to feel in a way that the camera could capture, I found a deep well waiting to be tapped. Performing onscreen was like opening up this faucet. I turned it on and—it was there.

Oh shit, I started thinking, if I had lines, I think I could do this. I could act. I could be an actor. I changed my résumé and put "actor" up front: actor/model/dancer.

I didn't know what I was doing right away, but over time I found that acting was a way to take my pain, doubt, and fear and project it all forward onto something else, to create something out of it. It wasn't just the work; it was the world of support that came with it. The arts community had proven

With a family
friend in our
apartment

In front of our
entertainment center

Communion

Mom and me

Flat top

With Ray
Thomas
during my
theater days

With Jeffrey
Wright
on the set of
*The Public*

Omar Little in *The Wire*

Chalky White in *Boardwalk Empire*

Freddy Knight in *The Night Of*

Montrose Freeman in *Lovecraft Country*

Shooting *Black Market* in Queens on the way to a gap house

An interview in Los Angeles for the Lean episode of *Black Market*

Interviewing a port officer for the *Black Market* episode on carjacking

Speaking to students
at Luis Muñoz Marin
Elementary School for
Social Justice in Newark
for *Raised in the System*

Talking to an Office
of Neighborhood Safety
(ONS) program member
in Richmond, California

Speaking with kids at Lucas County Juvenile
Justice Center in Toledo, Ohio

With Dominic and his brother,
Nolan, on the day of Dom's release

Celebrating at a Cracker Barrel

At a social
justice dinner
with rapper
Styles P,
local law
enforcement,
and community
youth

First block
activation
for We
Build the
Block in
Crown
Heights

Handing
out PPE in
Brownsville
during the
first wave of
COVID-19

itself to be my true home, opening its arms to me when I didn't even want to show my face.

That year, 1994, I got a call from my manager, Tracy "Twinkie" Byrd, about an audition for a Madonna video for her *Bedtime Stories* record. When I arrived, I looked around to see all these Fabio-looking boys with Greek god features, Spanish boys with perfect hair, beautiful white boys with Adonis bodies in tank tops, chiseled kids who lived at the gym. I thought: *I don't belong here. I'm a skinny, dark-skinned kid with buckteeth—I'm getting out of there.* I didn't even put myself on tape.

Twinkie called me back. "The casting director said she didn't get you on tape."

"Yeah," I said, "I don't think I belonged there, there were—"

"Michael, they *want* to see you! You don't know if you don't try."

She was right. And I booked the job—it was for Madonna's "Secret"—but I was scheduled to go on tour for three weeks with Crystal Waters, so I had to choose. I respected Crystal, but it was really no choice. A Madonna video was a Madonna video and the exposure—and the doors that would open—was just too much to pass up.

A COUPLE YEARS AFTER I first learned what *emote* even meant, my headshot was spotted by Tupac Shakur. I got hired for his film *Bullet*, playing his younger brother. On-set, Tupac was a force of nature. There was all this activity circling him but he had this calm center, like the eye of the storm. He had a presence and aura that I haven't seen in anybody before or since.

I remember one time waiting for a shot to set up, and he sat down near me. He told me the story of how he picked me. He had seen a picture of me at the production office and saw that I had a scar on my face. "Who is this guy?" he asked. "Go find him. He looks thugged-out enough to play my little brother."

He told the director—Julien Temple—to give his character a fake eye and an eye patch like Slick Rick, so we were an aesthetic match. We each carried our damage right there on our faces.

I was extremely intimidated by Pac. He was just larger than life. He took up space in this palpable way that you can't teach. I can't say how well I got to know him. I learned a lot by watching him, but you didn't do small talk with Tupac. He wasn't the kind of guy you sidled up to to talk about the Knicks or the weather. Either you had something to say or you shut up. I spent most of my time quiet around him, watching, listening. He was a man on a mission.

I remember one time they called him to set but the crew wasn't ready. "Next time you call me," he said calmly, "be ready, 'cause I'm ready." Then it happened again. Then it happened a third time and Pac lost it. "I told you, mother-fuckers! I come to set ready to go!" And then he stormed off. Everyone froze. Maybe I wouldn't go about it the way he did, but I took the lesson. Don't show up and then start to get ready. *Come ready.*

The whole *Bullet* shoot terrified me, but it was the good

kind of scare. I hadn't really learned how to inhabit someone else—that would come later. In fact, because of union rules, my dialogue on *Bullet* was dubbed over. But the exposure, and the work the appearance did as a résumé line, was huge. It's still crazy to think about it: my biggest mistake got me my first acting gig. I cannot make sense of that sequence of events, but I try not to question it too much. It all seemed to happen according to some mysterious larger plan.

Though *Bullet* was my first film, it didn't feel like my first acting job. That would come from a visionary artist named Matt Mahurin. I was on my way to a dance rehearsal when I got a phone call from Matt's production office. Matt had seen my face in something and wanted to shoot me for the poster of his movie *Mugshot*.

When I got to the photo shoot, I was trying to tell Matt, "You know, actually, I'm an actor, Mr. Mahurin," but I'm not sure if he was paying me any mind. I imagine photographers hear a lot of posers (and poseurs) talking about their acting dreams. However, I had a lucky in. The casting director and the first assistant director on Matt's film actually already knew me from some music videos we did together. When Matt showed them my picture, the casting director said, "Is that my baby, Mike Williams?"

Matt asked me to come in for an audition. In the movie, the character's name was Rumor and he was in a gang that wore all black: black button-down shirts, black neckties, black trousers, black shoes, along with white leather jackets. They went around the city as neighborhoods were gentrifying and robbed white people. My character carried a camera and the gang would traumatize victims by making them think we were going to kill them. Then we'd photograph them in that state and put it in a scrapbook.

I borrowed a white leather jacket from my friend to wear and headed for the production office. On a sidewalk-meltingly hot day in July, I rode the train in all black with the white leather jacket, people looking at me like I was insane. I walked down Seventh Avenue South in the Village, where the office was, near Christopher Street. It was strange being back there on my old stomping grounds where I hung with Robin and Darlene, past clubs where I first came into my own, near the cigar shop where we used to buy our blunts. I was back there but this time auditioning for a movie, part of the future that Robin had predicted. That was the first time the full circle felt so strong.

After I booked the part, Matt and I met at a diner in the West Village. Over turkey sandwiches and chicken noodle soup, I answered his questions: personal ones about my childhood, my family, even what my bedroom looked like. I was so excited about booking it, my first main role, I hadn't put much thought into actually having to do it. The first day on-set was like a wave cresting and then burying me. The very first shot was just me. Matt's costume designer, Hollywood, a short white hippie chick in a sundress, was getting my wardrobe ready for the first scene. I had nothing to pull on to prepare myself emotionally for what the role demanded, so I started to lose it. I went into a corner and crouched down and started to hyperventilate and panic: What am I doing here? I can't do this. I'm gonna fuck this up. I don't know what I'm doing. Holly came over to me, grabbed me by the collar to lift me up, and open-hand smacked me in the face. "Don't you go there, Michael!" she said, her eyes burning into mine. "Don't you do that! Fear blocks the flow."

*Fear blocks the flow.*

I snapped back, stopped crying, and thanked her. After that, I felt like I was ready.

It was an emotional process, tapping into that character. It was all new to me, and I didn't really have the tools yet. Later in the movie, I tell the rest of the gang I want out. But you never get out. I was hiding out from them when they found me, ran up on me, and held me down on the sidewalk. They Krazy-glued the jacket on me so I couldn't zipper out of it and the leader took a white marker and wrote his phone number in white ink on my forehead to deface me. A way of saying *I own you, motherfucker.*

My character goes back to his apartment, cuts himself out of the jacket, and washes the ink from his face. As I was staring at my reflection in the camera, washing the ink off, something hit me. Staring at my face—not the ink but the scar that would forever be there—I just lost it. I actually allowed myself to feel and I just emptied out, like a dam broke open. I broke down in that bathroom.

When I came out, sobbing, Matt just grabbed me and hugged me. "I love you, bro," he said. Then he told me to go home, wrapped for the day. It was the first time I let myself go through the trauma of being attacked, and it happened at a time when all these eyes were on me. Five years had passed since I was cut and I was finally dealing with the trauma—of nearly dying, of staring death in the face like that. How I'd always be staring death in the face.

If you push something down, it'll find its way out. You can't run from it. Jay-Z says we can't heal what we never reveal. And it's true.

*You can't heal what you never reveal.*

I had put it away expecting it to vanish. But pain doesn't work like that. It lingers. And when you don't look at it, when you don't let it out, it only gets stronger. And that's how it takes you down.

# CHAPTER 10

# ART + LIFE

AROUND THE SAME TIME OF THOSE FIRST FILMS, I
started to take acting seriously as a craft, worked to immerse
myself in it the way I had with dance. I grinded and hustled,
beat that pavement, landed a few film and TV auditions,
found my way into the Off-Broadway theater community. I
met talented and hungry and passionate people working it
where the lights shone less brightly. Their kindness and grace
made room for me even before I knew what I was doing.

It began unexpectedly. One evening I was walking back
to the D train in the East Village from a day of background
work on *NYPD Blue*. I was wiped out, carrying my bag of
clothes (you brought your own) through rush-hour foot traffic, a little aimless, looking to unwind. I remember thinking,
*Man, if I had just a blunt right now, all would be good.*

Then a voice from within the faceless crowd: "Hey, Mike,
what's up?"

I looked over at a stairwell and saw a light-skinned gentleman around my age, the smell of reefer wafting over from him and his friend.

"Remember me?" he asked, gesturing to himself. "Ray Thomas. I was in that play with Earl. Remember?" I couldn't place him but maybe faked like I had. "Come join us," he said, which sounded fine with me.

Ray remembered me from a play reading I did with a modeling friend of mine named Earl Nash. Earl was the full package, a Bronx kid who was cocky, athletic, and talented. In our modeling days, he was already looking on to bigger things. I asked Earl once about what kind of modeling campaign he was looking to land, and he said, "Modeling? This isn't even my forte. I'm an actor." *Forte?* I thought. *What's this guy talking about?* But I didn't say anything at the time. I could see that Earl was an ambitious dude and he dreamed big. I liked being around people like that.

Earl once asked me to come to his apartment to run lines with him for an audition he had. I read my part—straight off the page—but when he started speaking, his voice seemed to be coming from somewhere else, from *someone* else. He became another person right there in the room. When the scene was over, I had my jaw on the floor.

"Yo," I said, "what the fuck did you just do?! What'd you just do?" It shook me; I had never seen anyone do that before. I remember thinking: I want to learn how to do that. It was straight magic.

So Ray remembered me through Earl. Ray had this high-pitched, calm, smooth voice, glasses, manicured Afro. I'd call his style hood conservative. Over that blunt we got to talking and he told me about his coming up from Philly to work with La MaMa, an experimental theater run by legend Ellen Stewart. We were actually sitting right outside of the place— Ray had just finished for the day—and his energy and enthusiasm about working there shone through.

Ray and I became fast friends. He introduced me to the world of theater and became something of my spirit guide. He selflessly opened himself up and poured into me, shared his love of the craft and his belief in my talent. Around Thanksgiving, I told Ray, "My family is your family. You're here by yourself, and you've shown me so much love. For Thanksgiving, come break bread with my family at my crib."

When the day came, Ray hadn't shown up. Then I got a call from him.

"Where you at?" I asked. "We're about to break bread. Where you at, bro?"

"Yo," he said, calmly but directly. "Listen to me. I need you to get on the train and come to the city right now."

I took the train into the East Village, to the La MaMa Theatre. Ray greeted me at the door and walked me inside to where Ellen Stewart was sitting in an audience seat surrounded by all the producers. She was a distinguished Black woman with a big smile, flowing white hair, and a lilting Cajun accent. Stewart was already in her mid-seventies at that point, a living legend. She was holding my headshot in her hand when Ray brought me over. She looked me up and down, looked back at the picture, and said two words I'll never forget:

"He'll do."

I didn't know what was going on, but Ray explained to me that he and Ellen were going through artistic differences.

He was moving to a smaller role but incredibly, after losing the job, Ray recommended me to take over his old role. It was a wildly selfless thing, a great opportunity, and I was too green to even realize it.

"Excuse me, uh . . . Michael," Ellen Stewart called from her seat. "When can you start?"

I took Ray aside. "Ray, who's this crazy lady? It's Thanksgiving. Let's go back to my crib and break bread."

"No, no, no!" Ray snapped. "You're gonna stay and you're gonna do this! And I'm gonna help you." I admit I didn't even know Ellen Stewart, much less understand what a big deal she was. This also was going to be her last directing job to cap off an iconic career. Ray stubbornly made sure I knew and talked me out of my foolishness.

I stayed that night for two hours for my first rehearsal—I was behind and there was so much to learn. The play was *Tancredi and Erminia,* what Stewart called a "city opera." Ray would meet me at La MaMa every day and rehearse with me. It was highly technical: I had to learn the lines, the music, the choreography, the fight choreography with swords, and how to do that specific kind of musical singtalking. It wasn't like Luther Vandross, but it still took practice. It required a discipline that I had not yet honed, and Ray helped me get into that space. I remember one of the teachers at La MaMa, Sheila, who taught me the music. She had cocoa-brown skin, long braids, and a loud, raspy voice. When I would try to sing, she would hit me in the gut and say "Michael, bring it from herrrrre!"

Without Ray's help, I would not have even been in that room, much less made my way through the production.

After, Ray and I did some other work together. He co-created Theater for a New Generation (TFANG), and he and his mentor—director Mel Williams—would have a group of young actors up from Philadelphia come join us. Ray would find small spaces for us to rehearse in, black-box theaters to perform in. I started to do weekend workshops with them and slowly but surely, they brought the program to New York City permanently.

The next year Ray called me up again. "Mike! Listen, brother, get on the train and come to Harlem!"

By that point, I knew to listen to Ray, so I did as I was told. He met me outside the National Black Theatre (NBT) and said, "I want you to audition for this role."

"Which one?"

"It's for CJ. The same role that I'm auditioning for."

I looked at him, like *what?* I mean, who does that? Bring me up there to go for the same role? In his mind, we were communal, not competition. To him, my getting it was like both of us getting it. Ray was an angel in my life. I still don't understand the selflessness that he displayed to me; I still ponder it. Some people gain strength by giving to others and Ray was one of the first people in my life like that. To this day, he's never even brought up how much he did for me, never asked for anything in return. Never once. If I do mention it, he'll downplay it immediately. Ray showed me how to share love and resources, pouring into me for no other reason than I was his brother.

I booked the role of CJ, and again Ray ran my lines with me. He taught me how to memorize, showed me that a great way to get intimate with your dialogue is to write the entire script out by hand in pencil, how important it is not just to know my own lines but my costars' lines too. It lands differently. In theater especially, you're dependent on other people's cues because it's all live; there's no cut, reset, action. It's a dance. One person cannot be off, or the whole thing will be thrown off-beat.

Ray and I would sit over a game of chess and a bottle of wine, jazz playing in the background, and he would speak into existence the entire life that I live today. Of all the things he gave me, his confidence in me was the most important. "You know, Mike," he'd say, "I can see you with a bunch of scripts in your hand, working two jobs at the same time, have a couple of Emmys . . ."

Ray imparted his love for theater, which is different from television or film. Hollywood doesn't admit it, but theater is church. Those places, especially the old ones, have their own particular smell, like cathedrals—it's embedded in the wood. There are spirits in those buildings. The room is alive. It's tangible, textured, present. Theaters carry that smell and that spirit. It's in the floors, in the seats, in the rafters.

The play at NBT in Harlem was called *Endangered Species* and it was written by Judy Shepherd-King.* It was about young Black men, violence, and the trauma that comes with being immersed in that life. I reconnected with Earl Nash, my old modeling friend, the first actor I ever saw disappear into a role. He was one of the leads, and I would watch him backstage getting into character. There was one particular scene where he's broken and loses everything, and I watched

---

* Judy's son is writer/director Shaka King (*Judas and the Black Messiah*).

him channel his pain to get into that space. This was all new to me and I studied it intensely.

My way in was Biggie Smalls, whose *Ready to Die* album was released a few months earlier. On my Walkman, back-stage, I put on headphones and turned it up:

> *It was all a dream, I used to read* Word Up!
> *magazine . . .*
> *Every Saturday Rap Attack, Mr. Magic,*
> *Marley Marl*

That Biggie album spoke directly to me as I sat in the dark corner of a room in the back of the theater, meditated on these songs, and thought about my neighborhood, on the people I've been and the people I'd lost. I felt like he was talking directly to me.

My relationship with music is a huge part of me. Growing up I knew all the disco records, soul records, those early rap records, I loved all that. When, in the late 1980s, groups like N.W.A hit—I'm not going to lie, that stuff scared me. I remember the first time I heard "Fuck tha Police," I got frightened. *Oh my God,* I thought. *The police are going to start kicking my ass in the street.* With my dark skin, jeans, and sneakers, I knew I'd be targeted. I made a conscious decision at the time to change the way I dressed, to look a little bit more like a club kid. I also saw the birth of hip-hop getting actually violent, when it started getting personal. I remember the beginning of the Biggie/Pac feud. I was there for all of that. I watched that be born and happen right before my eyes.

My twin nephews, Dominic and Nolan, who were teen-agers at the time, would accompany me to the rehearsals, hang out at the theater, stay for the shows. Though they were considerably younger than me, they showed up for me in a big way. Our mothers were very close, and whether it was visiting me at Daytop, taking me out, or supporting me in the theater, they made sure I didn't feel alone. They under-stood what *Endangered Species* was about, the pain and the trauma that it was speaking to. A couple years later, they would understand it all too well.

There's a scene in the middle of the play where my char-acter runs behind one of the sets at the back of the theater, up to the stage, to break the news that one of our friends got shot and killed. The lead actors of the play, Earl Nash and Gano Grills, would actually switch roles every week. The first time I ran up on the stage to tell Gano about his friend being killed, he forgot his lines for a moment and he looked at me, moved to tears. I threw him. After that, I was hooked. *I like this level,* I thought. I wanted to home in on that depth.

The experience was a type of therapy, a form of processing my trauma, and a relief to release it all. Whether tapping into my own assault a few years earlier or the memories of losing friends, it was healing. An important aspect of the experience was who we were performing *for*. Harlem came out in droves—I don't remember one empty seat. To be able to do that in a room full of my people, who intimately knew that world, understood it on a cellular level, was powerful. I'd reach out to the audience up on those risers and they would receive me. Night after night they would receive me—in the church of that theater.

———

DANCING WAS STILL PAYING the bills, so I hadn't given up on it entirely. I was working as a background dancer on a tour with recording artist Maya when my manager called me up in California. She told me that Martin Scorsese wanted to meet me for his new film and that I had to get back to New York by Monday. I told the musical director that I had a "family emergency." I'd later joke that this was no lie, because if I didn't get the part it was going to be a family emergency. I borrowed money from a friend and got a flight back home.

I booked the part in the film, *Bringing Out the Dead*, though I admit I felt a little out of my element on-set. One time Nic Cage, Tom Sizemore, and Marty were standing having a conversation between shots and I wanted to walk up and be the fourth grown man in that circle, but I stood back, feeling inadequate. Though that was on me. Marty went out of his way to say hello; I was the one who would just shrink.

I had one scene, but it was a powerful one. My character is a drug dealer who's been shot in the chest and is lying on the sidewalk. Nic Cage plays an ambulance driver who pulls up on me as I'm bleeding out, dying, and loads me into the ambulance. My character is terrified—realizing he's going to die—and asks Cage to hold his hand.

Lying there, trying to invoke the horror and fear of dying, was the first time as an actor that I channeled something. In my mind, I went back to the death of my friend Maurice, who I watched die seven years earlier outside Vanderveer. I was coming home from the movies and I saw his girlfriend hysterical in the alleyway off Front Page. I double-parked and got out and Maurice was there gurgling and taking his last breath as she was screaming, hovering over his body. On-set, I got inside of that memory somehow, what it must have felt like, what it looked like, the body language of what I saw him doing before he died. I didn't even have to think about it; it just came to me. It was an instinct. I tried to channel the fear of what he must've felt, as his life slipped out of his body.

I felt like I honored Maurice, like I told his story. He didn't die out of sight, ignored or forgotten or barely mentioned in the back of the newspaper. His death mattered; people would pay witness. It was an opportunity to show the world what his final moments were like.

When Marty yelled cut, Nic Cage looked at me with tears in his eyes. "Wow," he said. "Wow." Then he walked away.

I never went back to dancing after that.

When I started training with Mel Williams and Ray Thomas in the theater, one of the main things I learned was to play to the back of the room. You want the people in the back row to feel the same performance that the front is experiencing. The energy will make its way from the back to the front row up to the stage, not the other way around.

After a few years in the theater, I internalized that lesson. But when I would go in for TV and film auditions, it was considered too much. I did an audition for casting director Alexa Fogel for HBO's *Oz*, a gritty prison drama that predated much of what became known as "prestige TV." Alexa emphasized to me that the camera doesn't need you to project like that. "Michael, I'm right here," she said. "It's all right here. Stop playing to the back of the room. The camera will bring you there." I didn't get the part, but the audition was fortuitous. I would stick in Alexa's mind for something else.

I landed a guest appearance on *Law & Order,* and then an episode of *The Sopranos.* At the time, in its third season, *The Sopranos* was just about the biggest show in the world. The plot line involved Tony's daughter's boyfriend, who was hiding out from mobsters in my apartment with my daughter, killing time and playing chess. The show wasn't known for its dimensional portrayal of Black characters, but I liked that I was a father raising his own the best he could. It was a small part, but just being in that environment was intoxicating, a rush. I felt like everything was starting to fall into place. I put myself out there, had dropped the dancing track to pursue acting, and the momentum was building. It was all on the upswing.

AND THEN—NOTHING. CRICKETS. The problem with burning fast and bright is that it can go away just as quick. I felt like I had found my way onto this carousel and then one day, it just stopped. I couldn't book anything if you threw it at me. The parts vanished, then the money, then my confidence. I began going into auditions anxious and desperate to get one scene, one line. It wasn't effortless, it didn't flow. Going in there with the wrong energy, like my life depended on it, felt off. Things turned dark, negative; I reached a point where I thought maybe it was over.

**KENMORE QUAD THEATRE**

**FLATBUSH, BROOKLYN, 1999**

In the spring of 1999, I was still living in Vanderveer, down to my last dollars, striking out on every audition. After getting some weed to roll up in a blunt, I didn't have enough money for a movie ticket and a van ride, so I walked to the Kenmore Quad Theatre on Church Avenue in Flatbush. The film was *Life*, with Eddie Murphy and Martin Lawrence, about wrongfully convicted men who spend their entire life in prison. I went in for a laugh and came out with something else.

About fifteen minutes into the movie, gunfire erupted in the theater. The second I heard it, I got low. I didn't even have to think about it—there was no freezing, no shock, just my hood-honed instinct to get on the floor. On my elbows, with my torso rubbing the ground, I crawled out of there like I was in a war zone. I got stepped all over as people rushed out, but that seemed like a better choice than getting shot. It's messed up that "get low" was something that I just knew to do in that situation, that I had known since I was young, like how to hopscotch or play stickball. It was just another example of the way my community has normalized something so dysfunctional.

I made it outside, and in all the chaos I realized that the blunt had fallen out of my pocket. My finances were low enough that I couldn't just let it go. As I started to walk back through the crowd, pushing my way in, I noticed a young woman screaming, looking for someone. The two of us were the only ones swimming upstream against the flow of traffic, and I rode in behind her. We got back inside the theater and I passed her to look around on the floor where I'd been sitting. I found the blunt and put it in my pocket. Embarrassing to say, but I was relieved. As I turned back around, I saw the young woman, kneeling on the floor, a young man's lifeless body right next to her. To this day, I can still call up that image, still can hear her screaming.

Back outside, I watched from the sidewalk as the paramedics came out pushing the gurneys. As I put the blunt to my mouth to light it, I looked down at my hands, and they were shaking. I hadn't even realized it.

That kind of situation was so normal to me, but my body was telling me, *No, Michael, this is not normal.* My shaking hands was my body telling me that. There's the trauma of life in the projects, and there's the survivors' means of processing it. This kind of violence is so rampant, so habitual, that we put on blinders just to get through the day. We normalize the abnormal.

There's another level to this story. Without meaning to, in the way I told this story over the years, I contributed to that normalizing. I used to tell this story as a joke. *You know, I almost lost my life at* Life, I'd tell people. I even used to make jokes about my hands shaking too much to light my blunt. In the process of working on this book, I was telling the story to my nephew Dominic, and his face just went flat. It landed differently for him—because of what he's been through. "Yo, I never heard that story," he said. "That's fucked-up."

Of course he was right. But in order to deal with trauma, you either block it out or absorb it in a way that doesn't cause too much static.

It turned out that the murdered young man was a twenty-one-year-old aspiring musician who just happened to get caught in the crossfire; the young woman crying over him was his niece. He was a bystander whose only crime was standing up and running instead of hitting the floor like I did. It could have easily been me. In a split second, I went down; he went up. That's it. That's how quickly it happens.

If I was killed that day, would I have been written off as some aspiring actor and dancer with a drug problem? Would anyone care? Would people judge me if I got caught by a stray bullet? This young man's potential was never realized because of the randomness of this violence. It doesn't kill drug dealers or gang members. It kills people.

It kills *people*.

IN THE LOBBY OF our building at Vanderveer, there were two vacated office spaces that my mother converted into a daycare center for the community. She retired from seamstress work and opened it up around 2000, going above and beyond, mentoring young mothers, providing a safe space for local children, offering a free lunch program. Mom never turned her back on a soul, and that daycare center was the culmination of a life of being there for people.

With the acting gigs drying up, I took a job as an administrative assistant at the daycare, helped her set up computers and change diapers, just earning my rent money, treading water. This went on for a year or so, through 9/11, which felt like the end of the world itself in New York. I remember watching the towers fall from my roof at Vanderveer and then walking around the city for weeks afterward among that acrid smell. That smell of death and destruction just hung in the air, depending on the direction of the wind shift in the Brooklyn projects.

That winter, I was hanging one night with my friend Sean and my cousin Danny in my apartment, smoking weed, drinking beers, playing chess and spades. Both were married at the time, so they would come by to let loose a bit. We had the TV on mute and the music blasting. At some point, I looked up at the television and saw myself looking back at me. I almost did a double take; they were airing my *Sopranos* episode.

I froze, thinking, *What's wrong with this picture?* I took in the scene in my apartment: I was smoking weed, thinking about getting some cocaine (I was off the wagon again), working at a daycare, and there I was, on the biggest TV show in the country. My life had been on one trajectory, and at some point I turned the corner and was back here, to square one. Like I'd just run one big loop and hadn't gone anywhere.

I'm a big believer in signs, so I took it as an omen, a voice calling out to me: *Do you want this? If you want this, Michael, go after this.* My destiny was smacking me upside the head. *You're just going to throw it away like that? What are you doing here?*

It was fitting, having that moment through the television. TV kind of raised me, like a friend who was always there. To this day I like to fall asleep with the television on because it's comforting. So many key moments of my life happened through the TV screen. It's played the role of oracle more than once. Watching *Soul Train* and wanting to dance, watching *The Odd Couple* and wanting to be best friends with Oscar Madison, the life-shaking influence of Janet's "Rhythm Nation" video, the dream personified when I saw my peers in Michael's "Remember the Time" video. Now it was me, popping up on *The Sopranos*, asking me what the hell I was doing with myself.

I had no choice but to answer.

I went to my mother and told her I was going to give acting another shot, one *last* shot. I asked for a $10,000 loan, which—to her credit—she gave me. She saw I had that fire burning still, and though she maybe didn't approve of my path, she wasn't going to keep it from me. Not now. The first thing I did was go out to the Queens Community College computer show to build a computer. Back then if you didn't have the money to buy a proper desktop computer, that's what you did. You walked around the auditorium and bought separate pieces, flea market–style. Then they would build it for you out of the various generic parts.

I put together a new package: fresh résumé, new headshots on the fancy Kodak paper, and a new acting reel. I arranged it all with some small items from Tiffany, like pens, sprayed it with cologne, and sent it off as Christmas presents to ten key contacts in the industry. In my mind, it was like *I'm back*.

Then I waited.

And waited.

And waited.

I heard just about nothing back—my friend Jimmy gave me my one meeting—and the depression kicked in hard and fast. A few months later, my mom was knocking on my door about that money. "That was a loan, Michael!" I don't think she wanted the money back as much as she was trying to motivate me. But I couldn't get out of bed. I felt like I took a gigantic swing and missed. Fell right on my ass. The sense of failure was overwhelming. And slowly I came to terms with how it just wasn't going to happen for me. I'd work for my mom at what had become a successful family business, and that would be it.

By early 2002, I had accepted my fate when I got a call from the daycare center from my mother. "Come down here, Michael," she said. "There's a fax for you."

I had been off the grid, not going to auditions, not making or taking any calls, but one person had been trying to track me down. Alexa Fogel, the New York City casting agent, remembered me from the *Oz* audition. She had been scouring the city for me.

Alexa found the number of my mother's daycare and sent me a fax. I went down there, over to the fax machine, and lifted up that single sheet of paper. It was for an audition for a new show and the breakdown for a character.

His name was Omar Devone Little.

# CHAPTER 11

# OMAR

IF IT LOOKS REAL TO YOU, IT FEELS REAL TO ME. ON *The Wire,* Omar's tenacity and swagger were based on people I knew and grew up with—including Joanie's brother K— and Robin. But his pain, his raw nerves, I didn't have to look anywhere for that. I was built out of that stuff.

Omar Little was described as a guy from Baltimore who robs drug dealers, though he doesn't sell or use. He's gay, doesn't hide it, and operates as something of the Robin Hood of his community. My habit for auditions at the time was to go dressed as the character. For the *Wire* audition, which Alexa Fogel put on tape in her office, I wore a pair of my Sean John overalls over a New Jersey Devils hockey jersey, which Robin let me borrow. The scene was the one where me and my lover, Brandon, are followed into the graveyard by Detectives McNulty and Greggs. (I wore that exact same outfit when we shot the scene.) The scene shows Omar's power because even though the cops are following him, he's the one who leads them there. He knows they're tailing him and brings them there to have a parlay—on his own terms. I was channeling Robin there, her bravado, the ease with which she did not give a fuck. In later years, I loved telling people that one of the inspirations for Omar was a beautiful lesbian girl from the hood.

Alexa talked about how the goal for the actor on camera should be to condense all of your energy and have it ooze out through your eyes, like a pressure cooker or a steam kettle. The goal is to keep the intensity there, and let stillness be your best friend. Your face doesn't need to do too much because the camera will pick that up. On the show, when Omar was on-camera in extreme close-up, chin to forehead in the frame, I'd go as still as possible, so any little thing would jump off the screen.

If I'm honest, at the Omar audition, I was so beat down emotionally that the stillness came from somewhere else: I was just dog tired. I had given up and didn't care anymore. That's the most ironic thing. That exhaustion, that fuck-the-world attitude, helped get me the part that would change my life.

To play Omar, I tapped into the confidence and fearlessness of people I'd known growing up. I borrowed from the projects, even asking K— to take me up on the roof of my building at Veer to teach me how to shoot a gun. I'd held guns before, but never in preparation to use one, and I didn't want to be one of those dudes holding their gun all sideways. Concerned about my tiny wrists I asked K— to show me the proper way to hold one. "So, do I use two hands or one?" I asked him.

"Nothing to do with your wrist size," he said. "You definitely want to use two hands, because that's how people who know how to handle a gun do it."

We shot at the roof's steel door, the echo exploding into the air, the force of the recoil surprising me. We started with a 9mm, a small but powerful gun, with a kickback strong enough to knock you down. Then we used some bigger ones. K— taught me how to cup the bottom, how to use the sight on the top of the barrel, how to aim below your target because the kickback will raise you up enough to hit it. I practiced at it, over and over. Omar *had to* look like a guy who knew how to use a gun. Without that detail looking real, nothing else would have flown. You can have the whole neighborhood yelling, "Omar coming!" and running for cover, but if I walked out there holding that shotgun like I didn't know what I was doing, I'd get laughed off the screen.

As for Omar's homosexuality, it was groundbreaking twenty years ago, and I admit that at first I was scared to play a gay character. I remember helping my mother carry groceries to her apartment and telling her about this new role that I booked. I knew from the jump he was going to be a big deal. "This character is going to change my career," I said. "But the thing is . . ." I hesitated. "He's openly gay." My mother is as conservative as they come, and I worried she would not be behind me at all.

"Well, baby," she said, "that's the life you chose and I support it." She hadn't embraced the arts or my interest in them, but to me, that was her version of encouragement. I took it for what it was worth. I think my initial fear of Omar's sexuality came from my upbringing, the community that raised me, and the stubborn stereotypes of gay characters. Once I realized that Omar was non-effeminate, that I didn't have to talk or walk in a flamboyant way, a lot of that fear drained away. I made Omar my own. He wasn't written as a type, and I wouldn't play him as one.

After getting over my ignorance of guns and my concern about his sexuality, a new, more potent fear dug its way into my mind: *This dude is a straight-up killer.* He strikes fear into the heart of anyone in his path. But everyone knew I wasn't that guy. People were going to be scared of "Faggot Mike"? They were going to run from "Blackie"? I was thirty-five years old when I started on *The Wire* but carried that scared childhood self close; he lingered under my skin, just below the surface. So the self-talk got fierce: *There is no way you can pull this off. You have nothing to pull on. There's nothing remotely you have in common with this guy. You don't know how to make him believable.*

The change came when I stopped trying to bring myself to Omar and started doing the opposite: I brought Omar to me. I dug into how he was like me, tapping into what we had in common. Omar is sensitive and vulnerable and he loves with his heart on his sleeve. You can say what you want to him—it rolls right off—but don't you dare mess with his people. He loves absolutely, fearlessly, with his whole entire being.

After clicking with that, I understood him completely. I came up with the narrative that his vulnerability is what makes him most volatile. When he cries and screams over his lover's tortured and murdered body, screaming in the halls of the morgue and hitting himself in the head, that looks real because it felt real to me. When Omar goes after Stringer Bell and everyone else responsible, he is driven by love and loyalty. Omar scared the hell out of everyone, but I played him as vulnerable, sensitive, raw to the touch. That's what I tapped into about him. He *feels*. But he's also an openly free human being who doesn't give a rat's ass what anyone thinks of him. And that gives him power.

I signed on for seven episodes, and considering Omar's "occupation," I figured he'd be done for after that. So I got serious. Shooting in Baltimore for Season 1, I was as sober as I'd ever been, barely even smoking weed. I treated the job like my life depended on it because in some ways it did; I came *this* close to not even being there. By that age, I'd been on the addiction/relapse merry-go-round enough to know how things could unravel once drugs entered the picture. I knew where they would lead me because it was always to the exact same place.

When I first got down there, I did my homework to learn the specific Baltimore accent. I remember sitting at a table at Faidley's, in the back of Lexington Market, over some crab cakes, and just watching and eavesdropping on people for hours. I picked up the interesting phrases, the habits of speech, the way those vowels sometimes took left turns. Baltimore has this character, like a stew, that comes from being part North and part South. Some things come up from Virginia and the Carolinas (where my dad's family was from), and some down from the Northeast. It all converged in Baltimore, meshed together, and became its own unique thing.

When I came out of the downtown market and—in

broad daylight—saw addicts nodding out right at the corner of Eutaw Street, I actually thought it was a setup for a shot for *The Wire*. I didn't know much about Baltimore, but that sight woke me up. It drove home what we were doing. I'd met some people, heard some stories, and learned that the life expectancy in the Black neighborhoods of Baltimore is worse than in North Korea and Syria. Part of my process involved walking around the hood to get a sense of what it was like, especially at night. I knew East Flatbush, but you can't just transfer one hood to the other. I feel like too many shows and films just do "New York" when they're trying to capture a certain kind of urban Black community. But David Simon and Ed Burns were definitely going for something specific. There are similarities—we're all human—but the character and textures are different, and I aimed to absorb what I could.

One late night I was driving around that area with a friend—windows down, sunroof open—and I heard some dude yelling what sounded like "Airyo!" After the second or third time, I pulled up at the curb and called one of them over to the window.

"What is that?" I asked. "What are you saying? 'Air-Yo'?"

"Where you from?" he asked.

"Brooklyn."

"What do you say in Brooklyn when you call each other?"

"Oh!" I said as it clicked. "You're saying 'Aye yo'?"

So I worked that into Omar's vocabulary. It's like "Hey, yo"—but "Aye yo," with a peculiar Baltimore *r* sound jammed in there that took some practice, as did Omar's specific drawl. I got compliments from Baltimore people on that, and when viewers were surprised I was from Brooklyn, that meant a lot to me.

Accessing Omar required my getting into a certain headspace. Music had always been a portal to take me into a character, and I would put on headphones and listen to these playlists I made (Omar's had Tupac, Nas, Biggie, and Lauryn Hill) that tapped into memories, emotions, places I wanted to access inside myself.

I found where Omar and I intersected, but he was also a fantasy of who I wanted to be. Not a thief or a badass, but an openly free human being who didn't give a damn, who took what he wanted, who wanted without fear, who loved without shame, and who feared not a living soul. Omar became an outlet for Mike. I was picked on so much growing up, and felt like such an outcast as an adult, that playing someone who was liberated from that, liberated me. It's why it was so hard to let go of him.

Once I put on that long black trench coat, lit one of those skinny clove cigarettes,* and heard "Action!" no one could lay a finger on me. Omar traversed his territory like it all belonged to him. Sometimes he snuck in through back doors of stash houses, while other times he just walked right down the middle of the street, whistling his signature tune. (The sound wasn't me but a woman they dubbed in.) I always thought of it as "A-Hunting We Will Go," though David Simon said it was "The Farmer in the Dell."

I also loved how Omar is the opposite of the stereotypical hood types. He isn't about the cars, clothes, and women. He

---

* Omar might've carried Newports, but I actually smoked Djarums.

doesn't fit into any of the boxes people might try to stuff him in, whether that's morally or sexually or something else. In so many ways, he stands alone. But he also feels pain, especially when his loved ones—Brandon and then, later, Butchie—are killed in these horrific ways. Both times the pain cuts even deeper since they are killed because of him, to send a message to him, because his enemies can't get to him. That's a particular kind of hurt.

A director calling "Cut" doesn't erase what you're feeling. Your mind feels the fictional the same way it feels the real. There are spaces in your brain—and your body—where there is no distinction between the two. If you activate trauma and pain, you don't have control once it comes out. And it comes home with you.

That's the flip side of getting into a character; you wake up that sleeping beast, those actual memories, those real emotions. I meditate on painful things all day long for a scene and when it's over, it's little wonder I'm tempted to go off and smoke crack. Drugs had long been a smokescreen, a cocoon, a means for me to hide from the real. In character, sometimes things get too real for me. More real than real, if that makes sense. I don't "disappear" into a character; I go through him and come back out. But when I come back out, I'm not the same.

IN REGARDS TO OMAR and his lover Brandon (played by Michael Kevin Darnall) it seemed like everyone was dancing around their intimacy issue. There was lots of touching hair and rubbing lips and things like that. I felt like if we were going to do this, we should go all in. I think the directors were scared, and I said to one of them, "You know gay people fuck, right?"

At some point, the issue boiled over for me so I went to talk to Michael before we shot a scene. "Yo, Michael," I said. "It's time to step it up with Omar and Brandon."

"What do you mean?" he asked.

"I'm thinking in this scene we should kiss."

"Okay. But—that's not in the script though."

"But it feels right," I said. "Don't it?"

"Maybe let's run it by the director and see what he has to say?" he suggested.

"Naw," I said, "I don't think we should ask anyone. I think we should just do it."

He was game. "Okay, but don't tell me when you're going to do it. Make it spontaneous so it looks natural. Just go for it."

They called us for rehearsal and the crew was still putting the set together, getting the lights and camera up while we ran through it. When I went in and kissed Michael on the lips, everyone stopped what they were doing and went slack-jawed. Twenty years ago, men—especially men of color—were not kissing on television. I don't mean it was rare; I mean it *did not happen*.

The director, Clark Johnson, was on a ladder and he said, "Whoa, whoa, whoa, hold up." He wasn't really watching the first time but just heard the lips smack and maybe sensed the crew's reaction. "Do that again."

We ran through the scene and kissed again. "You're some brave motherfuckers," he said. "All right, let's get it." The crew all stopped what they were doing and rolled action. I think he was anxious to get it before one of us changed our minds.

When I got my first scripts for Season 2 and I saw the storyline had switched to white workers on the Baltimore docks, I was livid. Probably with a little chip on my shoulder, I sought out David Simon, who had more than enough on his plate. "David," I asked him, "I wanna talk to you. Can I come by the office?"

"Sure, Michael, come on by."

To his credit, he heard me out. We had a conversation, and I told him my thoughts—about this being a Black show about the Black experience that foregrounded Black actors and now it looked like he was changing all that.

"You know, Michael," he said. "I understand, but you need to trust me. If I lead off Season 2 going back into the low-rises, it's going to make your world seem very small."

Of course he knew what he was doing, and eventually I'd see the big picture: how the circumstances of Omar's world, his allies and enemies and victims, were connected—in some ways parallel—to the rest of the city's institutions. But I'd be lying to say I got that right away. That didn't come until I started watching Season 3.

At the time, I didn't get it at all. What I got was high.

THE BLAME RESTS ON no one but me—my addiction is what it is—but the dark world where Omar resided was part of what led to my relapse. I also know that circumstance— more money and more time—played a role.

It's like this: In Season 1, I was a recurring character, which meant logistically that for my shooting days, production would bring me in on an Amtrak train, put me up in a hotel, and then send me home when my work was done. Season 1 felt like: *Make the most of it, make your mark. Don't fuck this up.* But when Season 2 rolled around, Omar had become this breakout character and I was made a series regular (with a salary bump), so things changed. Logistically, I was required to move and live in the location of the production.

By then, I had fallen in love with Baltimore. That city just touched me. I've never loved a place more than Brooklyn until I moved there. My blood was there, and I had some connection that I can't explain. But I was financially illiterate, so I thought I was rich. Never mind agent fees, manager fees, taxes, and so on. I rented a beautiful apartment on the first floor of a brownstone in a nice area of Baltimore: two bedrooms, two baths, a basement, backyard, fireplace, exposed brick. I filled it with all the furniture from my Brooklyn apartment. It was the best quality of life I'd ever lived, and I had given it to myself. That meant something.

I could've thought ahead, saved that money, and just gotten a small furnished room in Baltimore, but I wanted to go all in. That place felt representative of the commitment I'd made in my heart. I had hopes of moving there, making it my second home. At least I had the foresight to keep my apartment in Vanderveer and pay the rent for the year in advance. Later, when the season was over and I had to do my auditions in New York, I could have a little place to crash.

As a series regular in Season 2, I was getting more per

episode and getting paid for every episode produced, whether I was in it or not. So I had more money *and* more time on my hands: it was the devil's workshop. My demons had room to *play*. On days I wasn't shooting I started getting high on crack and cocaine again and I rolled like that pretty much all year, until I was completely broke.

When Season 2 wrapped, I felt the thud of coming back down to Earth. I could no longer afford the rent on that beautiful Baltimore apartment. Putting all my things in storage, I moved back to New York, to my empty Vanderveer apartment, which had nothing but a mattress on the floor and a milk crate to eat on.

When the rent came due again, I had nothing left so I got evicted. I had nowhere to live and my mother was trying to get me to go to rehab, but I was not having it. It was like admitting that I had fallen back.

My mindset at the time was that if I didn't treat it as true, maybe it wouldn't be. But she knew. She always did.

# CHAPTER 12

# HIDING OUT
# IN NEWARK

*A man gotta live what he know, right?*

—Omar Little

OMAR BECAME A SUPERHERO COSTUME I WORE TO hide from myself. I put it on, made it my own, and then let it overtake my life. The lines got blurry and it all went to my head. Everyone thought that I was him, and pretty soon, I was making the same mistake. Inside that long black trench coat, I felt invincible, protected from any threats from the outside and whatever was haunting me on the inside. Not only did I not have to be Mike, but I could be someone revered, feared, and beloved. Everywhere I went people wanted to buy me drinks, smoke me up, or just shake my hand. People confused me with Omar, which I became all too happy to accept, and then I confused myself. After I went home for the day, or even wrapped on a season, I didn't change out of my costume. I wasn't ready to get a look at what was underneath.

When I first left the cocoon of Vanderveer as a teenager, Robin had christened me Kenneth, a dude who was stronger and freer than Mike ever was. Now I had been renamed again, on a much larger scale, and I embraced the hell out of it. Omar seemed like the antidote, the answer to everything I had been hiding from. And what made all of it so much easier to feel like that was the drugs.

Cocaine was there when I was feeling good about the person I was pretending to be. Crack was there in my darker moments, when the seams started to rip, when I felt vulnerable and this voice would creep up on me, asking: *When is the other shoe going to drop? When are they going to find out you're a phony? When are all your secrets going to be revealed? When are they going to turn on you? Will they love you when they know who you actually are?*

DURING THE HIATUS BETWEEN *The Wire*'s second and third seasons, after getting kicked out of Vanderveer, I was essentially homeless. Fortunately, I booked a couple of film roles in Los Angeles (including the film adaptation of *Lackawanna Blues*) and was put up in a hotel through production.

While I was out there, I became friends with a dude named Malik. "Yo, Mike," he asked, "can you get me a part on *The Wire*?"

I liked Malik and he had been helpful to me out west, so I gave him a real answer. "I can maybe get you an audition," I said. "But if you're not a local hire, they probably won't look at you." I told him to move to Baltimore and he'd be welcome to crash with me there, but I needed help with a car. "No problem," he said. "I'm gonna call my cousins from Jersey. They can hook me up."

Malik never came to Baltimore, but a few months later I met up with him and his cousins in New York City. "Yo," he said, ringing me up, "we coming in from Jersey to go shopping. Come meet us."

I waited on Madison Avenue near Barneys and saw a flock of them pull up to the curb, a Nissan Z and a Benz. It was, like, soundtracked and run in slow motion: these dudes with long beards and jewelry stepped out of those cars, flossing, like they owned that street. They just inhabited their space like royalty or something. This was my first encounter with the Hill brothers, a large family of six Muslim men who had a construction business in Newark and a reputation as the OGs of their neighborhood.

I was doing a *Law & Order* episode at the time, staying in a Midtown hotel. I'd swing by the Hills' Newark place, and they welcomed me. They would throw parties, and I'd disappear into the loud music, the free-flowing Hennessy, the tight brotherhood. After enough times of me coming across the river to party and stay late, they began to say, "Yo, Mike, you might as well spend the night." Then when I had nowhere else to go—my bad habits had landed me broke again and *The Wire* was between seasons—they invited me to move in.

We became like family. I felt like people were wanting things from me, so hiding out with the Hills felt safe. They let me live there rent-free off and on for months and I'd sleep on the couch in the basement with their pit bulls. A brother would bring me down my halal breakfast with a blunt, we'd read the paper together, and then he'd go off to work. During the day I'd let the dogs out, cook when I could, help keep the house clean.

"Relax, man," one of the brothers told me. "Be yourself, you good."

"You want me to be myself," I said, "you'll let me clean this motherfucker."

The experience was humbling, which is probably what I needed. I was just one of them. They didn't care about my being on television, though they called me "O," as everyone did at the time. The Hills were like a fence circled around me, protecting me from those who might want to get a look at Omar crashing in their basement. They didn't want the community knowing I was there, figuring it'd attract too much attention, sensing I needed some time with eyes off of me.

I say it was like a brotherhood because we were close, but to be honest, they were more like father figures. They were positive, strong, nontoxic male authority figures—maybe the first ones in my life. I took to them like they were water in the desert.

They ran that block, made sure it didn't get taken over by a gang, made sure the crack and heroin dealers didn't hang around there. Meanwhile, one of the biggest fiends that side of the Hudson River was living in their basement rent-free. They had no tolerance for hard drugs, so I had to sneak off to do my thing. I felt guilty about it, was afraid they'd kick me out if they saw my full true self. They loved me, but I wasn't comfortable laying out all my demons. So I was hiding out from the people I was hiding out with, latching on to that old addict self. He was familiar, comfortable like an old blanket, and I wrapped him tight around me.

One time I disappeared for a weekend and drove everyone crazy. I was with this drug dealer in a crack house and told her to hold my cellphone because people were just ringing it, constantly looking for me. I couldn't handle it. That was reality on the other end of that phone and I wanted nothing to do with it.

"Make any calls you want," I told her. "Just don't answer it if it rings."

The first time the phone rang, she picked up. "This ain't Mike's phone no more," she said, and hung up.

The Hill brothers heard that and thought I'd been kidnapped. They flipped out, loaded up in their cars, and drove around everywhere looking for me. After they found me, strung out and scared, it was harder for me to hide who I really was. The seams had split open and something had to give.

Robin was living nearby and saw I was struggling. Once again, she stepped in, just like when I was a scared thirteen-year-old afraid of his own shadow, a seventeen-year-old coming out of his shell, a twenty-year-old crack addict kicked out of rehab and needing somewhere to land. We could go years without talking but she was like my guardian angel; she knew when I was in trouble and she'd always just show up. Robin tried to help me by bringing me to God. First, she took me to Pastor Mary, but that didn't work out. As Robin said, "Her church wasn't good for you. They just smacked you over there. What you need is to get punched in the face."

Next she took me to Reverend Ron Christian at Christian Love Baptist Church in Irvington, on the Newark border. Reverend Ron was a *survivor* who'd been in jail, had been through countless rehabs and detoxes for cocaine and heroin addiction, and who didn't turn his back on a living soul. Stately, with a bald head, caramel skin, and black horn-rimmed glasses, Ron was a literal godsend. Here was a man who'd had his own sordid past, who didn't judge me but met me where I was. He understood that connection between pain and strength and accepted me for who I was.

I once heard the saying *I've never met a strong person with an easy past.* Those who have been through the gauntlet survive for a reason. Reverend Ron opened his arms to everyone, *anyone,* no matter what they did. Sometimes that involved convincing them to turn themselves in to the police, soothing them in their time of grief, giving them food or money or a sense of community, or helping them into rehab. The Rev was a beacon of light and I credit him with allowing me to come to terms with myself. He helped me get to the root of all my fear, addiction, and self-destructiveness by listening to me, embracing me, and introducing me to his faith and his community. That church became my sanctuary; it was exactly what I needed and I didn't even know it. The Hill brothers had been father figures trying to keep me in line. But Reverend Ron became the mother figure I needed to keep breathing.

I poured my heart out to him and he didn't judge me.

Never, not once. I was high sometimes around him and he knew—addicts *know*—but he wouldn't shut me out. When we spoke, I felt known and, more important, seen. It's hard to explain the kind of effect that had on me.

Reverend Ron was a living example to me that one's past doesn't define their future. Your flaws are not disqualifying and everyone is worthy of love and forgiveness. "I've been right where you've been," he told me. "But I didn't have to stay down, and you don't have to neither." Though he had this genial, calm center in private, up on the pulpit he was a thunderbolt. He had this electric, God-speaking-through-him, sweating-through-his-shirt dynamic energy up there.

Despite all those years at church with my mother and my time as an altar boy, I never really felt a connection to any spiritual force, certainly nothing I'd call God. I kept Him at a distance and didn't get a relationship with a higher power until I was nearly forty years old, and it was because of Reverend Ron. He tore down my preconceived notions, let me see that *You can't see God until you go through something.* He didn't mean God as some supernatural force up there in the sky. He meant that force with you, within you. He would lift me up in that church and tell me, "Mike, I'm gonna love on you until you learn to love yourself."

It didn't happen right away, took years in fact, but Reverend Ron was the beginning. I started to see myself as worthy of his love, of that congregation's love, of God's love. It all started there in that New Jersey church.

It's not like *boom* I was saved and clean all at once. There's not an addict on the planet who it's like that for. Being an addict means forward and back constantly. It means saying no again and again. That's why someone who is clean for thirty years can still call himself an addict. They're always one choice away.

ONE LATE NIGHT AT a club in Baltimore, I was drunk at a table when I heard last call. Not wanting to wait for the waitress, I stumbled to the bar to get one more shot of Hennessy. Standing there, I looked over and saw someone who stopped me in my tracks. I thought, *This is either a young pretty boy or a masculine-looking woman.* I couldn't take my eyes away. She was androgynous and stunning and her energy was the loudest thing in there.

"I'm a female," she said, sensing what my question was. I thought she was beautiful and there was this magnetic pull coming from her, like we were meant to know each other.

"Okay, I got you," I said.

"What's up, yo?" she said, recognizing me. "I heard you were repping my city."

Her name was Felicia. We got to talking and I encouraged her to come down to the set of *The Wire* for an audition. *The Wire* was always interested in authentic, and Felicia "Snoop" Pearson was as authentic as they come. She had lived that life, had scored in it, had suffered in it, and soon enough she was portraying the fictional version of it that was based on her own reality. I think I introduced her to the *Wire* co-creator Ed Burns, but the rest of her story is all on her— she's a rare talent and powerful presence, as real as they come.

As she and I became friends, I learned more of her story. Born premature to a crack-addicted mother, she was raised in East Baltimore by her foster mother and father. As a teenager she worked for local drug dealers, was arrested at fifteen, and served six and a half years in a maximum-security prison. She was charged as an adult for second-degree murder for shooting a woman who attacked her with a bat during a street brawl. When she got out, she tried to go straight, but she kept missing out on or losing jobs because of the violent crime on her record. So she went back to making money in the streets, which is what she knew. Then we found each other. I *know* our lives were meant to intersect. Her presence on *The Wire*, the way it gave her a voice and a platform, was yet another thing about that show that was so much bigger than television.

As the years went on, I got out of my own head and came around to see that *The Wire* was bigger than Omar, bigger than Mike Williams, bigger than Baltimore or even just the Black community. David Simon knew what he was doing. The show, which added to its world each season, was creating a portrait of America.

I remember the day toward the end of Season 3 when we shot the scene where Omar kills Stringer Bell. It ate at me, and I avoided Idris Elba, who played Stringer, all day. I was troubled by it, the message. Why is this the way two Black men settle their differences? It bothered me, especially since Stringer was making his way through college, setting up in real estate, trying to get out of the game. And I had to kill him.

I talked to the writers about it, about why that had to happen. Dramatically, for story purposes, I understood. But as a Black man who felt he was representing his community, it bothered me. There was a larger problem than maybe I could articulate at the time. But it stayed with me.

*The Wire* was real in the sense that those characters whose lives were in the street could be killed off at any time. That's how it really is. Guys like Stringer Bell get killed. Guys like Omar Little get killed. The realism of that world demanded that Omar too meet his fate. So when the time came for him to go, I'd had enough preparation. But it was not easy.

Omar is killed unexpectedly, buying a pack of cigarettes, by a young kid in the streets. It's not played for dramatic effect—there's no slo-mo, no music. It's even early in the episode; it's just something that happens, just as it would really happen. (Even his body tag is mixed up in the morgue.) The actor who played the shooter, Thuliso, was ten or eleven at the time. We rehearsed it, but during the run-through we didn't set off the squib, that small stick of dynamite on my clothes. The first time he saw the effect go off was when we were rolling; that scared look on his face you see onscreen is the real human being, the real little boy going into shock. He drops the gun and is freaked out; that's not acting. We all stepped right into the real there.

After they yelled cut, he started crying, bugging out. "Is he all right? Is he all right? Michael?!" I had to console him. We had to wait awhile to make sure he was okay to finish the scene. Other setups were needed, and I had to lie there in that pool of blood. I'd died onscreen before—and I would again—but lying there, as Omar, was different. It felt like the end of something.

That day, when word got out that *The Wire* was shooting in the neighborhood, and that it was an Omar scene, the corners got packed. They had to cloak me behind a hood and robe so the onlookers couldn't tell I had been shot in the head. That kind of information would get leaked; people would pay good money to know that. I'd actually get calls sometimes with people offering me money to tell them upcoming storylines so they could make bets about who was going to get killed on the show.

During a break that day, I went to the trailer and one of the wardrobe people, Donna, came in to change my shirt. She saw me sitting in front of my vanity mirror, headphones on, spacing out, listening to Tupac's "Unconditional Love." I was going into a dark place and she could see it all over my face. "Unh-uh, no," she said, "we're not doing this today, Michael. We are *not* doing this today. Snap out of it."

I met her eyes and came back, but I couldn't avoid it forever. It was strange energy on the set that day. People were trying to avoid having any feeling about the show coming to an end. People had come to like me and adore Omar, and there was this resistance, like no one wanted to allow themselves to feel. It was very businesslike: *We got a job—no one's got any time for that shit. Jobs begin and jobs end.* That was a practical choice; we needed to get through it. But underneath all that, something heavy was lingering. Especially for me.

Omar's death was also the death of something that had grown inside of me, something I'd grown inside of, merged into. That was a crippling realization. I remember thinking that if I wasn't Omar anymore, then who was I? I had defined my worth through this fictional character, and now I was just Mike again. I felt stripped, lost, emptied-out. It was like this darkness crept in on me during the end of that show.

In Philadelphia, Mayor Michael Nutter hosted a *Wire* finale screening party at city hall, with a huge projector, screen, and crowd. Afterward there was a panel for cast members and I sat up there in a pitch-back Boy Scout shirt, pulled my baseball cap low, and didn't really speak. They'd ask me questions and I'd ignore them. I was too far inside myself to say a word. I didn't even want to hear my own voice.

I might've looked like I was being difficult, but I was just afraid. It was like in *Forrest Gump* when he decides to stop running across the country and everyone following him just kind of stops too and wanders away. I felt like one of those people. Like, *What do I do now?* It wasn't even about the next job. It was *Where do I get this feeling again? How am I going to reach in and get that feeling?* That drug, that Omar drug, that shit was *powerful,* and I didn't have any legs to stand on. I didn't know who I was because I had stopped doing work on myself. I was getting high and putting everything off. As I wrapped on *The Wire,* I knew I'd have to deal with the last four years of my life, having done whatever I wanted, damn the consequences.

I had been working on myself in my twenties, building resilience, spending time in recovery, facing my addiction head-on, being careful about who I let into my life, and I'd let go of all of that. Omar became an excuse to live however I felt, indulge in immediate gratification, but there was always a part of me keeping score. I knew that bill was about to come due. For my last scene, I was lying on the slab in the morgue for hours, thinking: Okay, now I got to get back to work.

Not too long after, I remember blacking out in front of my mother on Halloween. I had been up for days, an exhausted mess, my body was beat-up. She fed me some dinner and said, "Mike, you want to go upstairs and get some rest?"

"Nah, Ma, I want to sit down in the TV room with y'all."

She protested. "But the trick-or-treaters are going to be ringing the doorbell."

"Ma, I've been up for days," I said, closing my eyes. "I don't think a trick-or-treater is gonna wake me up. I don't want to be by myself right now."

There was nothing that could've been scarier at that moment than being alone.

# CHAPTER 13

# INFLUENCE

*Everybody's at war with different things.*
*I'm at war with my own heart sometimes.*

—*Tupac Shakur*

**HARRISBURG, PENNSYLVANIA**
**2008**

WHEN I PICKED UP THE PHONE, I HEARD MY MOTHER struggling for breath.

"Ma," I said, panicked, "what's the matter? What happened?" I thought something was wrong with her or maybe someone had died. "Ma? Ma! What happened?"

Her breath broke through, heavy and loud. Turned out she was laughing. *Hysterically* laughing. "I'm watching you on TV," she said, "giving advice to some kid about keeping himself straight!"

"Yeah? Wow, you scared me, Ma, I was—"

"And he's got a—he's got an ankle tracker too!" Her laughter was punching into my ear.

I hung up, furious. But she was right. It'd be funny if it wasn't so terrible. I'd have laughed too if it wasn't about me.

Three months earlier I shot an episode of *Judge Hatchett,* a court TV show that sometimes did a special episode where entertainers intervene in the lives of at-risk kids who've been through her court. Judge Hatchett contacted me to go on the show to meet with a fifteen-year-old boy from Shreveport, Louisiana, named Marquawn. Marquawn had gotten into some legal trouble because of his sticky fingers, and a judge had put an ankle monitor on him. I took him around New York City while they filmed us for a day. I brought him to my neighborhood, then took him up to the National Black Theatre in Harlem and talked about how the arts saved my life, how dancing and then acting offered me an outlet that kept me out of the streets. I took him around and said, "This is where I started to find other things to interest me besides getting into trouble and doing drugs."

"What's with this ankle bracelet, man?" I said to him at one point. "You gotta get this off you! You gotta get living!" The segment ended with us skipping down 125th Street doing the Soulja Boy dance. Happily ever after. By the time the show aired, I was wearing an ankle monitor of my own.

Some role model I was. Mom found it too funny to breathe.

AFTER *THE WIRE* ENDED, I had put together a respectable period of "sobriety"—as in, no hard drugs. When you're an addict on a binge, you feel invincible until you break down. Then when you're cleaned up, you feel invincible again because as long as you're off the hard stuff, you figure you're okay. So I got sloppy and arrogant, far too comfortable smoking weed and drinking, assuming that as long as I didn't touch crack or cocaine, I was fine.

I was not.

After two DUIs in six months out near my mom's new home in Pennsylvania, I got up in front of a judge who was ready to throw the book at me. Facing ninety days in jail, I was dealing with my first legit confrontation with the law—I'd been busted for things like turnstile jumping, weed, and truancy when I was younger, but nothing too serious.* This was no joke and I'm sure I had it coming. When I went out to Pennsylvania to stay with my mom, I'd show up with my aggressive New York energy, bar hopping and drinking behind the wheel, and PA law enforcement was having none of it.

The judge slapped an ankle bracelet on me and sentenced me to up to 250 hours of community service. It was embarrassing; it was one thing to hurt myself, but DUIs endanger *other* people's lives. I was caught, humbled, and figured it was time to step up. I had seen the famous and privileged make a mockery of their community service hours and I had no interest in doing that. In my mind, the least I could do after getting sentenced to community service was *serve my community*. "I got in trouble," I said to my lawyer. "I was wrong. I don't want to clean toilets or adopt a highway, I want to make this meaningful."

---

* I might've once stolen a taxicab for ten blocks before getting stopped by cops, but that's a story for another time.

So I came up with the idea of going to high schools, speaking to teenagers who came from backgrounds like mine, sharing my story, my struggles with addiction. I wouldn't preach at them but come at them with the truth, let them know about the decisions I've made and the consequences I've had to face. I would be honest about the fact that getting in trouble with the law and needing to get my paperwork signed for the judge was why I was there in the first place.

It felt right, but I was nervous putting myself out there, having gotten used to hiding behind brash characters who spoke in ways I never could. Put me in a fictional scene with lines I had to memorize, and I could be anyone. But just Mike, all alone up there? That scared me senseless. Which is exactly why I needed to do it. I didn't know it yet, but fear is like the smell of smoke. It's usually a sign that there's something bigger there.

Being open about my issues in a room full of people was a way of telling on myself, maybe even punishing myself. It was time to pay up. And exposing myself was part of that process. I could reach out to kids who didn't know how to share their pain because they never learned that they were *allowed* to. Young men, especially young Black men, are taught that vulnerability is weakness, which is a dangerous and destructive lie. I'd give them permission to be vulnerable, show them that it's actually strength. True strength, not the hollow, swaggering kind. I warned them about what was lying in wait for them if they weren't careful. If they didn't focus. If they didn't dream. I know it was my dreams—in front of the TV, on dance floors, or on Manhattan's rooftops with Robin and Darlene—that saved me.

I was intimidated to get in front of those kids. This wasn't the silent comfort of the Hills' basement or the loving embrace of Reverend Ron or even an interview with a journalist who knew not to push too hard. I'm sensitive and didn't want to leave there with my spirit broken. You never know how people will receive you.

I also knew kids were skeptical of adults trying to feed them a line, would laugh you out of the room if you didn't come direct. If I was going to stand a chance, I had to come in with the unapologetic real. It couldn't be just me standing up there and expecting them to listen to me or identify with me because I'm on television. It was about me reaching out to them, identifying with *them*. The onus was on me to connect. I just hoped that they would see me.

The first talk was at a rough high school in the Bronx. Bracing myself for ridicule or judgment, I went in there hot, nervous, and just hoping they didn't laugh at me: *Look at this crackhead up here trying to tell us what to do.*

But something amazing happened. They listened.

I talked to them about staying off drugs, which I obviously knew nothing about, and I told them that. I didn't come at them from a place of authority or wisdom or expertise. Just experience. Just someone who'd been there. I tried to present my problems as a dose of reality about what substance abuse actually looked like. "Look at me," I said, "living the dream, on TV, doing what I love, and still drawn in by drugs and bad choices, living in this painful place. I don't even have my youth to blame." I knew, at forty-one, I was emotionally and mentally stunted, though I didn't say that aloud. I was still a child in my head, rebelling against my mom, saying fuck the world, making bad choices, hiding from what I didn't want to face. And I was still teetering. "I'm not out of the woods, and it can all disappear if I keep at it," I told them. "You don't get too many chances when you look like me."

By the time I spoke to a high school in Germantown, outside of Philly, I saw that I was needed, that I could contribute, be part of a mission. I was honest about growing up soft, looking for acceptance in what was available. I told them, "When I was your age, drugs, crack, were running rampant and I became a victim of that. Nothing to be proud of . . . but that's what it was. I let my education pass me by. I screwed up. I didn't have a plan B. I got a GED—a 'good-enough diploma.'" I said that last part with a laugh. I even did my homework that day, got my hands on some statistics about that particular high school's progress. It had gone through rough times but was on the rebound and I celebrated that. "These numbers are huge," I told them. "The city is watching."

They came up to me afterward, for pictures and autographs, some for just a hug. I felt their love. "These kids are never this quiet," one of the teachers told me. "*Never.* You don't understand, they're not like this when other people come to speak to them."

Kids are just looking for truth. If you give them that, I realized, then they are going to receive you.

I felt like I was redeemed through their eyes, though I wasn't yet at a place where I had forgiven myself. That would take a long time.

The power dynamic in these rooms was important to me. I never wanted these kids to think I was doing them a favor. It was not about me setting them straight. They were setting *me* straight. "I need to be here," I admitted. "I need you all to be okay. I need to know that you see me. I need to know that you see yourselves in me because I see myself in you all."

I came clean, apologized for being absent in my community, which I don't think a lot of people—especially men—in my position do. I don't want people to thank me for giving. I'm coming home. If I'm not doing that and investing in the youth in my community, what am I doing? I'm an addict who turned into an entertainer, so I haven't been around.

"I've been away," I'd tell them, "but I'm here now. What do you all need? Talk to me." I started asking them questions, finding out from students what career they were pursuing and then following up with the *how*. What were the tangible next steps? I know we can't be what we can't see, so the more I could do to help them focus on the reality of their dreams, the more I was being of service to my kids.

I call them "my kids," even if I don't know them or will never know them. I call it my community even if it's a place I've never been.

That's where my hope lies. I can go back into the community and say: I made some bad choices, but you don't have to do that. You don't have to get scarred up in your face and end up in endless rehabs and almost die and overdose to finally recognize that you're worth something. You don't have to go through all this pain, because there is another way. I know there is another way. Let me show you.

THAT SAME YEAR, 2008, the year *The Wire* ended, when I finally started to come clean about who I was, I got called out in a way I never would have expected. It planted a seed in me that would take years to grow. I didn't even know what to do with it at first; it just seemed ridiculous, like an out-of-body experience.

In January, then Democratic candidate for president, Sen. Barack Obama, gave an interview where he talked about how Omar Little was his favorite character ("not my favorite *person,* but he's a fascinating character"). It got picked up in the news, and everyone was telling me or asking me about it. First the shock—*This guy knows who I am?* The fact that I had portrayed someone that caught his attention blew my mind. Sure, I believed in the power of the arts but at this level? Even having a presidential candidate who watched *The Wire* was something.

But the next thing that came was shame, because of my own cluelessness: *Wait, who's this guy again?* My political knowledge was close to zero, and I was embarrassed about it, how checked out I was about politics and the issues affecting my country, my community. How do I not know about this guy? This Harvard-educated dude with the African name and dark skin who might become president? What had I been *doing* with myself?

Obama saw me and I realized that I wanted to know what he was about, how I *should* know what he was about.

One evening when I was visiting my mother, she sat me down at the kitchen table.

"Let me talk to you, son," she said.

"What's up, Ma?"

"Mike, I'm proud of you, boy. You out there. Put the family on the map. Got Obama talking about you. Don't you turn back now."

I DID A VOTER-REGISTRATION drive for Obama in Indiana and a few other political activities that got my feet wet before the election. In March, I was invited to a town hall Obama was doing at the Forum in Harrisburg, near my mom's house. I'd just come off a three-day cocaine bender and was whacked out of my mind. Shooting a movie in Rhode Island, I threw on a sport coat and jumped on the Amtrak and went down to PA. I got to this packed auditorium and one of the female campaign volunteers found me, pinned a HOPE button on me, and took me by the arm. "Michael," she said, "we would love if you would speak to the Obama volunteer who makes the most fundraising calls at the end of the week."

"Sure, I'll do it," I said, having no idea what I'd even say: *Hey, this is Omar. Omar calling. Thanks for your support?*

I was in the back searching for my family when a campaign worker got on the stage and announced over the loudspeaker: "Michael Kenneth Williams has just endorsed

Senator Obama for president of the United States!" The room went crazy and the next thing I knew all this Secret Service had circled around me and I was like, *What is happening?* It was surreal.

After Obama's speech, his campaign staff invited me and my family to come downstairs to meet him. After we all got cleared, we went through and waited for him to walk in. I was intimidated, meeting the future president of the United States. He was not just the front-runner at the time but a global celebrity, and it was wall-to-wall people down there. He came down the steps and my cousin's wife greeted him. "Senator Obama, I understand that you watch *The Wire* and you're a fan of Michael K. Williams and he's here to—"

"Where Omar at?" Obama yelled out. "That's my man! The man with the code! Where's he at?" He found me in the sea of the crowd and grabbed me, gave me the homeboy handshake into a hug and pulled me in. "What's good with you, man?" he asked.

"G-G-God bless you, bro," I managed to stutter out.

I couldn't even put my words together I was such a mess. Obama shook my hand, and I could see it in his eyes. He was like, *I don't got time for this.* He kept it moving. I was not in my right mind. I told people I was nervous, but I actually had lockjaw from too much cocaine.

I wasn't yet in the headspace to even make sense of meeting Obama, much less make use of it. I would meet Obama again a few years later—when I was more ready to embrace the kind of influence he had, and accept the kind of influence I could have. But not that day. I was nowhere near ready yet.

# CHAPTER 14

# THE WORLD BENEATH THE WORLD

*You can't help it. An artist's duty, as far as
I'm concerned, is to reflect the times.*

—*Nina Simone*

**YONKERS, NEW YORK
2014**

ON THE RIDE TO SET, I BUILT A COCOON AROUND ME.
With Nas's raspy voice punching through my headphones,
those early morning drives were like a meditation. I'd stare
out the window and find my way into that dark headspace.
Long before I even considered myself an actor, on my first
film, I learned by watching Tupac to come to set ready. *Come
in character.* I've made it my practice.

There's a flip side to that though. Getting into character
beforehand—coloring outside those lines—means having

him with you afterward. Once you open the gates and bring him into your personal space, he bleeds into other parts of your life. You don't get to just take him off at the end of the day like a costume, especially if he's tapping into something personal. He follows you home. And then he's there when you get up in the morning—or when you can't fall asleep at night. At some point, it gets hard to figure out where you end and where he begins.

In the winter of 2014, I was shooting *The Night Of,* an HBO limited series written by Richard Price and directed by Steven Zaillian. On the surface, the show was a crime drama, even a whodunit, but underneath was a story that touched on a lot of issues at the forefront of America: immigration, criminal justice, class, race, the drug trade, addiction, sexual abuse, and the trade-offs people have to make to survive. The story focuses on a young Pakistani man (Naz, played by Riz Ahmed) who is wrongly accused of murder and does what he has to do to survive while incarcerated in New York's infamous Rikers Island while awaiting trial.

In there, he meets my character, a former boxer named Freddy Knight. Freddy, an addict and lifer, is the white-hot center of the block's power structure, feared by the inmates, manipulative of the guards. He has made a name for himself, and a home for himself, in this hell on Earth. So adapted to his surroundings, Freddy even gets his crew on the outside to get him charged with another murder so he can *stay* at Rikers. He says it's to be closer to his family, though he's settled into his role and routine there. Freddy is full-on institutionalized. In it, and of it.

Freddy's a complicated character whose motives skirt that gray line. He helps Naz get in touch with his own power while also using him to help run his drug operation. Freddy is drawn to the young man, whom he knows to be innocent. "It's like I got a unicorn," he says. It's a line that captures both sides of their relationship; he's looking up to Naz while also *possessing him*. Not "I know" a unicorn; I *got* one.

Freddy was the intersection of a lot of things for me. In one of the many scenes that rubbed right up against my reality, Freddy slices a sexually abusive prisoner in the jugular, killing him. He also freebases right out of tinfoil, pipe to his lips, and nods off. The character stirred up so many issues for me that before the shoot ended, after around five years sober, I would cave in on myself.

All of my scenes took place at the prison, which was actually a set built in a warehouse in a remote part of Yonkers. To get there, I'd have to ride out of Brooklyn up the FDR Drive, to the Major Deegan Expressway through the Bronx, and then into Yonkers. That early morning ride, with the highway spooling out and the colors lighting up the sky, would stir up a lot in me. It was like a portal I had to pass through to transform into this hardened soul. To turn that Freddy switch on, I had to pull from something deeply personal.

Going up the Deegan was the exact same route I would take to Green Haven Correctional Facility, where my nephew Dominic was locked in a cell like a forgotten man. By that point, he had been in prison for nearly seventeen years, and not a day went by when I didn't think of him. The prison cell where he woke up every morning was sixty miles up that same highway. Sometimes it felt like light-years away from that Yonkers prison set; other times it was right there, like right on top of us.

Dominic is more a brother to me than anything. He's the son of my aunt Miriam, one of the "Goon Squad" who used to drink and laugh with my mother at our kitchen table, discipline me when I got out of line. Eleven years younger than me, Dominic grew up in Vanderveer too, resisted all the temptations and detours, and kept a good head on his shoulders. In the mid-'90s, while I was working in the theater and auditioning, Dominic—who was still a teenager—already had his life together. He was a conscientious young man who'd done missionary work in Mexico and Africa, gone to Bible college, helped to take care of his family, and—along with his twin brother, Nolan—had always been there for me during my rough patches.

But in June of 1997, his world would come crashing down. It happened, as so many things did, at the corner of Foster and Nostrand: Front Page. On a pitch-perfect summer evening, I drove around the block to buy a bag of weed. I was gone not fifteen minutes, but when I returned, I found the street blocked off in many directions and a crowd, police cars, the candy-red lights of cops and ambulances in the street, neighbors on the sidewalk.

"You heard what happened?" someone told me. "Your nephew is dead."

"Wait, what?" The words hit me like a bag of bricks. "Who?"

"Nolan," he said.

"Nolan, my nephew Nolan?" I asked.

"Nah, it was the other one," someone else said.

"Dominic?" I asked. I couldn't get a handle on what was going on and my heart went like a jackhammer. Everybody seemed to know something, but no one was saying the same thing.

"Nah, he was the shooter," a third person said.

"Wait, what. What?" I asked. "Dominic shot someone?" That didn't sound right either. "No way. You still got it wrong," I said. "You guys made a mistake."

By the time I tracked Dominic down I got the whole story.

On his way to a vigil for his pastor's sick wife, Dom passed a group of dudes in the street who were attacking his twin brother, Nolan. Dom grabbed a gun and brought it into the scuffle, where it accidentally went off, and a young man (also named Nolan, which caused the confusion) lost his life. Of course the loss of the young man's life was horribly tragic, but it was tragic for Dom as well. He wasn't mixed up with crime or drugs; he never looked for fights or trouble. It was just an accident. My nephew has always been the first to take responsibility, to admit he made a bad decision by bringing that gun there; but in my community, having a gun is just how you defend yourself. The other side has one, so you better have one too.

In my panic and desire to help him, I tried to convince Dom to let me hide him in North Carolina, but cooler heads prevailed. His conscience and his mother wouldn't let him run. The next day he turned himself in. Dom should've been charged with involuntary manslaughter—all the witnesses knew it was an accident—but without the resources or money to access justice, he was hit with murder and given twenty-five years to life. The DA actually offered a plea, but Dom's lawyer never brought it to him. Maybe in his mind, helping just another young violent Black man wasn't worth it. Who knows? So in a blink, because of a single mistake, Dom's whole life was snatched away. He was nineteen years old.

At the time of *The Night Of,* I'd been visiting Dominic for eighteen years, almost half his life, in these harsh and cold places. It's a sad fact that in my community visiting prison is a rite of passage, a weekend activity like church or ball games. Long before Dom was incarcerated, I'd been going to jails and prisons to visit friends who were locked up for selling crack or caught up in the swirl of violence.

When I was seventeen, Joanie took me to visit her much older boyfriend in prison and we'd sneak in weed tucked inside baby balloons. We'd bag them up the night before, sneak them through security, and she would pass them over as she kissed him. Or he'd say, "Mike, go get the white soda," meaning 7 Up, which was my cue. At the vending machine, I'd pull the tied baby balloons out of my underwear and slip them into the soda can for him to drink. Since the security guards would search him all over, even make him bend over and spread his cheeks, his only option was to swallow the balloons and shit them out later. In *The Night Of,* Naz has to do this exact thing to bring in drugs for Freddy.

Dom spent his first year behind bars in Rikers among some of the hardest people and conditions in this country. He was moved a few more times until he was transferred upstate to Green Haven. Our family at least knew where he was, were spared the anxiety of having lost him to the system. That alone tells you how screwed up our corrections system is. We were *relieved* when Dom was moved to a maximum-security prison.

To get to Green Haven, you go well out past the city limits, the commuter suburbs, the mowed lawns of Westchester County. You keep going north and the buildings start to get sparse and then you're in farm country, the SUVs turn to trucks and tractors, and land stretches out as far as the eye can see. Finally you come upon this fortress: rising stone walls visible on the horizon. Coiled barbed wire, guard towers where faceless men with rifles serve as a constant threat. Inside, it's white cinder block, white-painted metal, and—overwhelmingly—Black men.

After giving my and Dominic's name to a guard behind glass, I'd empty my pockets, get searched with hands and wand, be buzzed in, and led to the visitors' room. It's all hard angles, posted warnings, that too-bright headache lighting, and mirrors at corners so nobody gets surprised.

I'd sit and wait, surrounded by other families on plastic chairs at small wooden tables, vending machines and microwaves, a corner where people got Polaroid pictures taken. Then out would come Dominic in his green khaki prison uniform, all light and love, giving me a big hug. "Uncle Mike," he'd say with a smile, with his inextinguishable, courageous positivity. We'd chat about family, and he'd tell me about the program he'd started in prison to talk to men in there about healthy reentry and ask about my work and life.

When we'd say goodbye I would try to hold back the tears while he would flash that bright smile and say, "Love you, Uncle Mike." Dom was a fighter in a different sense of the word: he never let the darkness affect him, even when it might've been easy to do so. He'd lost a lot during those years. When Aunt Miriam passed away in 2014, they escorted Dom in arm and leg shackles to his own mother's funeral.

Dom's story also stood for me as a reminder and a warning: we are all just one choice, one bad decision, away from losing everything. We talked by phone a lot, especially during that time, and I spoke to him about Freddy in *The Night Of*, how I was channeling parts of his experience in that role. I wanted to be authentic, to honor him through the character, to empathize with his life on the inside from the inside. Though Freddy used his power mostly to work a hustle, Dom used his to mentor other men.

In his mid-thirties by that point, Dom spoke with a focus and an energy that was undeniable. We spoke about choices, about knowing one thing and doing another, either through forces or demons or habit. These things spoke not just to my character but to me. "Part of the insanity in prison," Dom once said to me, "is remaining in your own prison." I knew that idea intimately and brought it not just to Freddy but to myself.

The atmosphere on the *Night Of* set was heavy and intense. Shooting in the cold, low-light winter in these tight, dark spaces surrounded by hard stone and men in dark-gray clothes, I was like a time bomb. There was nothing there but a base-camp parking lot, a few trailers where you could be alone in a small space, and the prison set itself. So while we ate lunch or waited for the crew to set up a shot, we sat on those metal stools at wood tables right there on the cell block. Over time, it slipped under my skin because it *felt* like a prison.

As an actor, if I don't believe it, I have no business expecting anyone else to. There is no emotion you've ever seen me have on screen that was fake. I actually go there. Nowadays, I understand the effect that has on the human brain. Parts of my brain *don't know* that I'm acting. My body doesn't know that I'm acting. My walk changes. I see through different eyes, remember things differently—or remember things I forgot—and wake up with trauma on a cellular level. What shows up onscreen always comes from something real inside of me. That's always been the only way for me. I take parts that are close to who I am but sometimes they cut too close to the bone, to the white meat. Toward the end of the *Night Of* shoot, I fell on my ass, relapsed bad, and they had to shut down production for a day until they found me.

I was never a recreational drug user. I am an addict, and an addict is always teetering on that edge, one small step away from falling back in. Freddy triggered me because he used drugs to survive: to escape, to cope, to numb, to forget. It's a spiral all addicts are caught in. We're addicts because our shame and our guilt keep us getting high. Every addict, every alcoholic has a self-loathing; we bathe ourselves in that. It's the way for the addiction to keep us on the ropes, keep us connected to the darkness. It fuels off of it.

After I went off the grid, my manager, Matt, came out from L.A. and my friend Goli flew in from Paris to live with me, make sure I got to set each day, and hung around to keep me straight. The second I wrapped on the show, we flew out to Malibu to put me into rehab. It was a bare-bones place, a residential facility where I detoxed, lived with a roommate, and needed written permission and a sober companion to go anywhere. It was rough, but exactly what I needed at the time.

Then, as it does, the universe intervened.

WHILE I WAS IN REHAB, Matt got a call from the director Spike Jonze asking for a meeting. It's the kind of meeting you take no matter what, so I got a waiver from the facility, and Matt and I drove out to Santa Monica, a sober companion trailing us in his car. Spike had become creative director of a new cable network that Vice was starting called Viceland, and he wanted me to host one of its flagship shows. It would be a docuseries called *Black Market*, which took a look at underground and illicit economies and how people made their money when the system wasn't available to them.

It sounded amazing, and we jibed immediately on the issue. But my next thought was *Why me?*

Spike talked about interviews I'd given, stories I've told publicly, the persona I presented and how that all made me the right person for the show. "People love Omar," he said. "And they trust you. These people, they're not going to open up to just anyone." I think *The Wire,* and what that show portrayed, went a long way in giving me that credibility. I didn't feel like I'd earned it yet. I hadn't come to terms with my own worth in that sense.

I didn't say so to Spike, but I felt like I wasn't informed enough for what he was asking, like he gave me more credit than I deserved. I was an actor, not a journalist, and what did I know about all this? Spike's confidence counted for a lot though. What clicked for me was when he explained the show through what would become its tagline: *When the system fails you, you create your own system.* I thought of all my mother's relatives coming up from the Bahamas ducking immigration and navigating the ways to get a green card, the friends I knew who turned to drugs or crime because they didn't see any other way.

*Black Market* was about the systems that people invent outside the law. I learned about trades that exist on the fringes and the lives tied up in them. Each episode has me in a new city and sometimes a different country, where underground guides show me around, offer perspective on their way of life: carjacking in Newark, Lean in Houston, addicts and shoplifters in London. I'm no saint—I've gotten glimpses of these worlds—but I had no idea how they operated. Sometimes openly, sometimes with their faces covered and their voices altered, these people let us in, shared with me, and offered an entry into their world. It was important to me that we also got into the conditions that led these people to do what they do. We couldn't just capture the what and the how; we had to show the why. If you ask me, the why is everything. The why is how we reach across and understand one another.

When I began, I was too tight, focused on my actor "process," as though I knew what I was doing and was in control.

I'd spent my entire life—onscreen and off—playing someone else. So I needed help to get to that place where I was just me. Dave Laven, who directed most of the episodes, helped me to get there. When I slipped into the role, asked questions instead of pretending I knew, that's when it clicked. Letting go freed me. I started to talk less and listen more. I never judged and I never talked down—I opened myself to them so they'd open themselves to me. It was hard work, finding a place within the chaos of the cameras and sound guys to get them to see me and feel safe with me. I learned as I went, whether it was abalone poaching in South Africa, honey oil in Boston, or the water crisis in Mexico City. I opened my mind like a gate for people whose stories were unknown. The experience was like the best school I could've gone to, on-the-ground education. In a just world, *Black Market* would be part of the school curriculum.

Because of my recognizability I get to hear these stories. It's a privilege, and I can't just let them lie dormant. I carry them, in a very literal sense. But accumulating the stories and magnifying them is just step one. We have to do more. This is still America; there are still opportunities and education. You can still grind and work hard and become something for yourself. You don't have to fall prey to the traps that are clearly set for you. As grim as it may seem, there is light that shines through. The amount of potential I've seen in these streets is next-level. It'd be inspiring if so much of it didn't get wasted or turned toward the darkness. I met a twenty-one-year-old working credit card scams who was a full-on genius. "If you put two percent of this brain power to something legal," I told him, "you could do anything."

"We don't know no other way," he said. "We don't have anyone to show us. I've heard people say to me, 'Start a company' and I don't even know where to go to have that conversation."

Meeting these people whose lives and livelihoods are precarious stayed with me. Once the cameras were off, I couldn't just move on. I can't let what I've seen just roll off me like other people can. I'm not built that way. So when I stepped into these worlds, I would come out different, each and every time. I was staring at some hungry, desperate kids who didn't want to stay stuck where they were but didn't know how to get out.

On an episode we were shooting in Chicago about gunrunners, a twenty-three-year-old kid broke down in front of me. "O," he said, short for Omar. "O, take me with you. I'm tired of this shit. I don't want to die on these streets." He even took off the ski mask, revealing his face. His voice cracked and the pain just flooded out of him. About six months later, I got word that he had been killed. It's a death that haunts me to this day.

The moment with that young man gets to the heart of the show. Think about it from their point of view: why would they let us in with cameras and microphones, *putting their crimes on television,* unless they got something from the exchange. People love Omar, sure, but not enough to risk their livelihood, so what is it? They are talking to us because they need help. They're reaching out, and we owe it to them to reach back.

A key reason these young men and women are on the illegal path is because their access and education have been blocked off from the main valve. Their smarts were not valued or encouraged or recognized during those impressionable years. The powers that be ignored them. As kids, they were told from an early age they didn't have it. So when they do get good at something, they don't even think of it as smart.

*Black Market* didn't shoot all at once. In between various TV and film projects, I'd be dropping in and out of these worlds, which made the experiences all the more powerful, like a reminder of everything that's bubbling underneath the surface.

I WAS IN LONDON, shooting a film and a *Black Market* episode at the same time, when I got a call from a friend in Newark. Rev. Ron Christian had passed away. Fifty-one years old and he died at his church office in the morning, in the place where he helped so many people. The news just about broke me. When the person you think of as your guiding light goes just like that, it unhinges you. And I became unhinged.

Reverend Ron saw me. He believed in me. He didn't care who I was or what I did, just that I was a man who needed love. He valued me and helped me understand my own value. That man was everything to me, and not having him around anymore made me feel lost.

Soon after, I was up in Canada on a film set, where I had another serious relapse. In the haze of that, I remember getting on my hands and knees and praying, just let it spill. In that state, I kept saying one thing over and over again to myself: *I don't want this shit anymore.*

When I came back up for air, I knew this couldn't go on. Something had to change. And it wasn't going to happen until I changed it. I just knew, even inside those darkest moments, that the answer was elsewhere. I had to commit to something bigger than myself.

# CHAPTER 15

# VOICE

IN THE YEARS RIGHT AFTER *THE WIRE*, STARTING in 2008, I was sharing my story at high schools and connecting with young people, but it took me years to recognize the other end of that, which was political action. I was blown away that these schoolkids actually listened to what I had to say, but I hadn't thought of contributing on a larger level. I'd always felt like my voice didn't matter, and I am far from alone in the Black community feeling this way. What ended up happening around the time of *Black Market* was a mix of me seeking something more and that something more finding me. I'm a big believer in signs and paying attention to when the universe speaks. And at the time, the universe couldn't stop running its mouth.

In the summer of 2016, *Black Market* and *The Night Of* started airing within about a week of each other. Both shows explored issues of class, marginalized communities, criminal justice, and underground economies. I was doing press for both simultaneously, so a lot of the questions were on these topics and I wanted to be able to answer. By this point I had hooked up with the ACLU to be their ambassador for smart justice, but it was mostly a campaign where they used my face. I didn't know yet what I needed to know, and it felt like time to grow up. My good friend Jimmy had been railroaded by the justice system and put away for life. From jail, he was asking for my help, so I started by advocating for him along with Leeann Hellijas, who'd been leading the charge to get justice for Jimmy.

Michael Skolnik is a film producer turned activist whom I met through *Boardwalk Empire*. He understands that the power and visibility of celebrity can be leveraged to shine light on the needy and create momentum to make lasting change. I attended an informal get-together at Michael's house for about thirty people working with social justice activism, including Olivia Wilde, Rosie Perez, and Van Jones. We sat out on Michael's deck, ate Moroccan food, and talked about how to use our platforms to address these social- and criminal-justice issues. I was new to that world and aware that these people had been doing it a long time. I brought up Jimmy's and Dominic's stories, but I mostly listened. The next meeting a month or so later was at Olivia's place in Brooklyn, which was a bit larger, with more entertainment people and also Obama's senior advisor, Valerie Jarrett. Afterward, Michael and I walked about the streets of Fort Greene, Brooklyn, and talked.

"Will you help me figure this out?" I asked him. "I got

people going back in my family, friends, my nephew Dominic has been locked up for eighteen years. Jimmy's got nine life sentences. This shit is personal to me, and I gotta do it right." Michael agreed and we started to meet every week or so to talk about things I could do. I didn't want to be just a face. I wanted to get my hands dirty. Or, depending how you look at it, clean.

The capper was a meeting in September 2016 at the Obama White House among some heavy hitters: former attorneys general, major CEOs, religious and civil rights leaders, and other big-name activists. Obama was in his last year—the home stretch—and his administration had been doing important work in criminal-justice reform.

There's nothing like getting invited to the White House to make you feel like an impostor. Once the excitement wore off, that familiar voice kicked in: *Who do you think you are?* I thought of all the things I didn't know. I thought about my mother, who complimented me about first being on Obama's radar. But the end of that conversation? The last thing she said? "You know, when you're in these rooms, son, just smile and nod your head. Don't try to talk."

It's not just her.

I notice how quickly white men hook each other up—the old boys' club. It's so bred into our culture; you're a white man, you know another white man, you get this job or you get into that room. It's knee-jerk. And my response had been knee-jerk too: stay out of the way, be the "ni**er talent." Black people learn to speak a certain way around white people, and in any room with both of them, there's code-switching going on. I had to push against my own instincts to stay passive, to "shut up and dribble," so to speak.

I felt small, wondering what business I had meeting with the president about these things. Having him call me Omar and give me the homeboy handshake was one thing. Talking to him about a major issue that affected millions of lives, including those closest to me, was something else.

Just getting invited to meet the president means you must've done something to earn it, but I didn't feel that.

"Yeah, but I'm just an actor," I said to Michael. "Why do they want *me* to be there?"

"C'mon, Mike," he said, "this isn't just about being on TV. This is your personal life."

"Yeah, but, I don't . . . What do I know about this?"

"A lot," he said. "More than most people. You've lived it."

The White House meeting was about twenty-five people in the Roosevelt Room, a windowless space with a fireplace, oil paintings, and that grand wood table; I felt like I'd stepped into a history book. Michael must've sensed my nerves because he came over to me while we were waiting. "Relax, Mike," he said. "Remember what they say: those closest to the problem are closest to the solution."

*Oh shit,* I thought. The lightbulb went on in my head. *Maybe I do know something.*

Besides, I couldn't have hidden if I'd wanted to. They put me right in the middle of the table, across from an empty chair and I knew who was going to sit there. Obama came out of the Oval Office into the room and began taking ideas from everybody. He mostly listened and Valerie Jarrett took notes.

When it was my turn, I spoke on what I knew. "This is very personal to me," I said to the room, trying to squash the nerves, feeling all those eyes on me. "My nephew Dominic has been in prison for eighteen years, for a crime he committed as a teenager. He's mentoring men twice his age, and I want to honor him whenever I speak on this. Growing up, I saw family members, friends, locked up, killed, and have seen how this affects communities like mine, poor communities of color."

Later on, I thanked Obama for all the clemency work he was doing and asked him what he planned on doing for the female population that was incarcerated, because up till then it had mostly been men. It was really the first time I realized I had agency, a voice, a life experience that mattered. That's what I could bring to the table. I could use my visibility not to score drugs or get a table at a restaurant or even make myself feel better but to actually contribute. Do something.

What happened next was a snowball effect. People were responding to my interviews and my answers on these issues as if I knew what I was talking about. Charlie Rose was asking me when I was going to run for office. I started thinking about criminal justice more seriously, as a larger cause I could address in my day job.

I had a meeting with producers at Vice—Dave Laven, Eddy Moretti, and Matt Horowitz—and just started talking about those dinners with Michael, going to the White House, and people I knew personally who had been caught up in the system: my friends Jimmy and Daryl, Felicia (Snoop), my cousin Niven, and Dominic.

"Let me ask you something," Matt said. "When did each of your family and friends get into the system?"

I started going through each one—fifteen, sixteen, eighteen, fourteen, nineteen—and I realized: oh shit, they were all teenagers.

"That sounds a lot like the school-to-prison pipeline," he said offhandedly. It was a term I'd never heard before. *Wait, what? School-to-prison pipeline? What is that?* I was shocked that such a thing existed. How on earth can there be a pipeline connecting these two things?

I looked into what was meant by the pipeline. "When African American children act out they are treated not like misbehaving kids but rather like juvenile delinquents," former federal prosecutor Paul Butler wrote. He found that "sixteen percent of black kids are suspended from school every year . . . 70 percent of school discipline cases referred to the police are African American or Latino kids." In ways large and small in this country, we criminalize Black adolescence.

Studies have found that "after age ten, black boys were seen as guiltier than white children." Age ten, that's *fourth grade.* The misbehaviors that get a phone call home or a trip to the principal's office in white schools bring in the police for the poor students of color. That's the pipeline. They enter the system from a young age, and it doesn't have any exit ramps—just a pathway further in. The system defines who they are, what they can be, and what life they will lead. Because these are kids, it often starts small, with something the police have no business being involved with in the first place.

The United States has the highest juvenile incarceration rate in the world, "spending a total of $5 billion a year to keep kids . . . in juvenile detention. Even our closest competitor, South Africa, incarcerates its children at one-fifth the rate of the voracious United States." And once they go further into the system, two things happen: it's harder for them to get out and they learn how to become criminals. You are thirty-eight times more likely to reoffend as an adult if you are touched by the system as a kid.

We mistakenly call them correctional facilities, but aside from a handful of alternative programs, there's no correcting going on. Young people's time behind bars does nothing to help them. After experiencing that trauma, they became hardened, their souls darkened. They grow up to become men and women who do what they have to do to survive.

As I learned more about both the juvenile and criminal justice systems, I was reminded of all those jail and prison visits I'd made in my life. What struck me was just how regular it was. We have to take a second to process how messed-up that is. We have normalized the abnormal so completely we don't even realize it. Why was this part of Black boys' coming-of-age? Why are some things praised and aspired to? Why are certain things like serving time held up as a badge of honor when they only lead to ruin?

The crack epidemic that almost swallowed me up created a response in the white community, in the government, a clamping down on and imprisoning of a generation of non-violent Black men. This is what led to the incarceration epidemic of the 1980s and '90s, whose effects are *still* being felt.

The kids in prison now are the children of that first generation, the ones that Republicans and Democrats both labeled "superpredators," as if they were some bogeymen instead of just children.

What came out of my talks and meetings with Vice was *Raised in the System*, a documentary for Vice on HBO, conceived as a way for me to use my platform to bring attention to an entire generation of kids locked up behind bars. There were tens of thousands of juvenile offenders, mostly Black and Brown, almost all poor, who were being written off in America's detention facilities. And there were those like my nephew who went to prison at a young age and were now going through adulthood behind bars.

Dominic's narrative was the spine of the story. Instead of disappearing into the darkness, he turned into the very definition of a role model, running a program to help prepare men for reentry. It allowed each of the participants to come to terms with who they were and who they could be. They were all once young men who could've gone the other way.

Right now, another generation of Black kids are having their futures stripped away. They are being discarded before they've even figured out who they are. You may choose to ignore what's going on with these kids, but that's not because they don't matter. That's on you.

Everyone knows that our criminal justice system is broken. But before we look at the justice system in this country, we have to look at the juvenile justice system. It's the same river. We just need to start farther upstream. At what point in these kids' lives could they have been redirected into a different way of life? What can we do at these inflection points to divert them? We need to change the narrative.

Similar to the approach with *Black Market*, in *Raised in the System* I take a journey onscreen—what you see is me learning about this world, meeting with people who work inside of it every day, and me connecting to these kids. I started to think about what I can do—what *we* can do—to show them love, bring them in, help them before the system has too firm a grip on them.

These kids are demonized by people who know nothing about them and don't care to know. They are pronounced criminals before they have a chance to define themselves. We have given them nothing to hope for, look forward to, or dream about. If anything, we're the superpredators, snatching their lives away before we know what those lives can be.

As a whole, white children's gifts are praised and supported and their mistakes are treated as mistakes. Which is as it should be—for all kids. But for Black children, especially Black boys from poorer neighborhoods, it's the opposite. Their gifts are ignored and their bad choices are vilified. Adolescence is criminalized in neighborhoods like the one where I was raised. I've seen it in Brooklyn, how some neighborhoods hold block parties and there's not a cop in sight. Meanwhile, in my community, which basically *invented* block parties, originated the music and dance and much of the food there, block parties are often crawling with police or shut down preemptively. The best description I've come across for this phenomenon is from author Ibram X. Kendi, who wrote, "Harmless White fun is Black lawlessness."

SHOOTING *RAISED* BROUGHT ME into a world that left me raw; I hurt for these kids, was angry at the systems that had failed them, and I wanted to put their stories up on-screen. In some ways it was like a prequel to *Black Market*—meeting the kids who could one day end up in that world.

In Bon Air Juvenile Correctional Center in Virginia, a lockdown facility built in the 1990s at the height of the su-perpredator panic, I visited a barbershop school in the prison. I sat in a circle with kids in the program, and I tried to get them to share, feel, open up. As they told their stories, about violence and crimes and punishing sentences, they kept say-ing things that drove home how young they were. One young man kept referring to Christmases as a way to mark the passage of time. His mind still framed things around Christmas, just like any kid would.

I've seen the evolution of people, how it happens. No one wakes up and says they want to be a gangbanger or a drug dealer—that's the last stop on the train. That's what you do when you're drowning and reaching out for something—anything—to survive. By the time they get to the corner, there has been a series of things that led to that decision. No one wakes up at the top of the mountain and decides they would like it better down there on the bottom. They end up there out of desperation. We don't spend enough time exam-ining the wider picture, the steps that get them there. We don't tell that part of the story. And to tell half the story is to spread a lie.

They make their choices because of lack of options. I've watched it happen so many times, to my brothers and sisters and family and community. One of the kids in the barber school was a nineteen-year-old named Danielle. She grew up with an alcoholic father and addicted mother, dropped out of school in ninth grade, and had been in and out of the system since. At the impressionable age of fourteen, her older brothers and sisters would ask her to do illegal things that they didn't want to get in trouble for, and she would do it for them. They were her role models, so she did what they wanted, to fulfill what she saw as her role in this family, which was also dealing with the devastating effects of poverty. "Sometimes no light, no water, no food," she told me, "so I turned to the streets for real."

Danielle was reserved during the talk, a little shyer than the boys, adding "and whatever" to her sentences, almost like a form of protection. Later, I talked with her one-on-one in her cell, a tiny room with a plastic chair, a cheap wooden dresser, metal toilet, and the thinnest mattress on a thinner frame. The cinder-block walls had a lion and Mickey Mouse outline, a reminder that kids live here. There was a heavy green door with no knob, just a circle where a knob would be and a slim picture window framing the hallway. As we talked, she took a brush to the back of her head, her chunky digital watch occasionally beeping.

At sixteen, Danielle was charged as an adult with grand theft auto and then convicted of a subsequent incident of assault and gun charges. She was sentenced to a cruel and brutal thirty-three years. Thirty-three years. When I met her, she had already spent three years in that lockdown facility, which *didn't even count* toward her thirty-three years. Three years of life sleeping and waking up in that tiny room just flat-out didn't count. That said it all, really.

She admitted that when she first got in, she was "wild," knew that if she had been let out soon after, she would just go back to the streets. But she's developed wisdom behind bars, had the time and distance to reflect on those things, recognizing she wasn't yet ready back then to get out. A year for a juvenile is a lifetime. I think adults forget that. "I don't think I learned my lesson," she told me. "I *know* I learned my lesson."

In her three years on the inside Danielle had time to recognize the consequences of her poor choices. Isn't that what we want? Rehabilitation? But by the time she gets a chance on the outside to make use of it, she'll be in middle age. If she even makes it. She has turned a corner in her life, but the system won't allow for that. It had decided who she was and moved on. Do we think thirty years in prison is going to make her a productive member of society? Do we believe dumping this kind of punitive time on a child is just? Who does that serve?

Danielle had been working toward her GED in Bon Air, along with barbering and culinary school certificates as a plan B. She was about to be moved to the adult prison, where she was planning on taking college classes to become a pharmacist. This young woman, who had decades ahead of her behind bars, spoke about how most people had given up on her, but "I get stronger from it," she told me. "I'm going to prove something to you. That when I get home I'm not going to be the same person." She'd be the first in her family to go to college, and she was "going to chase it." Her voice cracked on that, and I had to keep myself from tearing up. Danielle spoke passionately about how she wanted to volunteer with kids in her community, because she's been through the world that she wants to keep them out of. Like a spirit warning them off a possible future.

"You have a very good mindset," I told her. "You don't make any excuses, don't blame anyone for your mistakes, you have a plan, goal, focus." She was inspiring.

I shared with her how growing up in Brooklyn I was real soft and got picked on a lot and Robin took me under her wing and basically did her best to make me be a man on the streets. Danielle reminded me of Robin; she had that same toughness, that same heart. The softness inside the hard shell.

The day I was there, she was packing her stuff to go to prison. To start day one. The female officers came in to search her and others were fighting back the tears as Danielle was cuffed in shackles and put in the back of the van. We watched it happen in real time.

IN TOLEDO, OHIO, I met Tyron, a sixteen-year-old struggling with drug use who'd been arrested on a weapons charge and put into a court-ordered rehab program. He had just gotten home after four months in a juvenile facility, and a progressive judge—Judge Denise Cubbon—was giving him a real chance to make good in an alternative program: Community Treatment Center (CTC). Judge Cubbon told me that in "keeping him in the community [rather than locked up], we are increasing the likelihood that the kid is going to be successful." Her vision is something that is sorely lacking in the juvenile system across this country, but I was grateful to see it.

The program teaches life skills, provides counselors and group work regarding communication and handling one's emotions, and offers ways for kids to get enough high school credits to graduate.

The program was something special, but that meant it was rare. It is exactly the kind of thing we should be investing in. Not just because it's the moral choice—though it is—but because we all benefit from the prosperity of our children.

Despite the assumption that we're locking up violent kids, "young people are far more likely to be arrested for minor infractions than are adults," data suggests. "Even in large, state-run juvenile facilities—ostensibly reserved for the 'worst of the worst'—the majority have been sentenced for non-violent acts." So we misjudge who they are and put them away, in traumatic environments they are not prepared for. Then, since we are "*increasing* the odds that they will commit more crime in the future, these institutions actually undermine public safety in the long term." We're sending them in as kids but they're coming out as criminals.

Tyron was lucky. But if he didn't cooperate with the program, he'd be put in a youth treatment center (YTC), which is basically a type of jail. So when I met him, he was right on the edge, staring down his last chance. Tyron was also dealing with his own trauma. During his months away, his best friend was murdered. The desire for him to retaliate was fierce, overwhelming even. That's what he's been taught; it is the language and currency of his world. Plus, he was in pain: that's why he started getting high. As an addict, I understood that in my bones. Walking the line is not something you decide to do once; you have to re-decide it, every day, every hour, every moment.

Self-medicating through the pain, battling with his single mom (a recovering addict herself), and being a father to a nine-month-old, Tyron had a story that was still unwritten. Even within the heaviness, there was such light inside of him, a natural charisma and sense of humor. When he mentioned he'd been writing rhymes, I asked him to share some, just being kind. But what came out of this kid's mouth left my jaw on the floor. Tyron's rapping skills are undeniable. This was a special and talented kid who maybe just needed someone—anyone—to see him that way. For a young person, a drop of that goes a long way. I've seen it happen so many times.

One of the battles with his mother concerned how she got sober: finding God. In the documentary, Tyron says to the judge he doesn't believe in God, and his mother walks out of the courtroom. On break, I came over and whispered to him, asked him to come with me to one of the lawyers' rooms. I told the co-director, Matt Horowitz, no cameras, no microphones in there.

"Listen, bro," I said to Tyron, "you cannot do that. . . . You have the opportunity to make it right with what you do with your fucking life, those are facts. You know how hard it is for your mama to get high and get clean in the same neighborhood? And to try to raise her son in the process and get back the time she lost? And trying to be a good mother to you? You know how hard that is?"

He was nodding silently.

"You got a child, right?"

"Yeah," he said, "nine months."

"When your son starts walking, are you gonna drag him to keep up with you or are you gonna slow down to walk at his pace?"

"I'm gonna walk at his pace."

"Well, it's the same thing with your mother. When you went and kicked her crutch out from under her foot, she doesn't know how to walk. That's her belief system, that keeps her going. Slow down for your mama; you gotta play this game. Play this game. Or this game is going to play you."

"Yeah, I got it."

Although obviously Tyron had a lot of support from these women, the lawyer, the judge, and the counselors, it didn't escape me that I was the only Black male adult in the room.

Later Tyron made an offhand joke about the lack of positive male role models in his life. The idea was almost comical to him. It just killed me that something so profound—and so easy for millions of kids—would be so off the map for him as to be laughable.

What effect can one positive role model have? What can the community be doing to divert these kids? Not all of them had my luck: a connected and dedicated mother and an arts community that welcomed me, scars and all. We talk until we're blue in the face about their choices, but what about ours? They can't make better choices until they *have* better choices. By giving them no healthy or productive options, we are responsible for their bad choices. If we want to talk about choices, how about we talk about society's choice to give up on them so easily.

Every single one of us is a work in progress. Children even more so. So when we lock up our children and turn a blind eye, we are at fault. Each one of them who ends up dead, behind bars, or on the needle is our failure. There are higher levels of PTSD in kids from some communities of color than *soldiers returning from war.* The right intervention or mentor or chance can change the narrative. And the more we see that story change, the more we believe in it, the momentum can upend all of our preconceived ideas of who these kids are.

Off-camera, I met Donald, a CTC worker who worked with Tyron. He told me what I was witnessing was Tyron already on the path to change, that "even four months ago this conversation . . . he wouldn't give you the time of day." The same things that made him persuadable to the streets, make him malleable to positive change. "We're planting those seeds over there . . ." Donald said, referring to the program.

I kept in contact with Tyron for a while afterward; I wanted him to make that record. I was trying to encourage him to go into the studio and lay it down. He was funny, talented, his fire was still burning. I wanted him to win.

Dr. Laurence Steinberg, a psychologist specializing in

adolescence, told me, "There's almost no one in the criminal system that didn't start in the juvenile system." Meaning we need to start there to make changes. Dr. Steinberg, whom I interview in *Raised*, renewed my understanding of the word "adolescence." Until my conversations with him, I had never really thought about what the word meant. We're all human beings and white, Black, rich, poor, we all cross through that stage. If you're a human being, you went through adolescence, which is just a scientific word for a time when you're doing dumb shit.

It made me think about things like how car insurance is so high for young people, especially for people of color. The price drops drastically at age twenty-five for a reason. Steinberg's explanation of the science even helped me understand my own bad decisions.

"Adolescence is like a second infancy," Dr. Steinberg said, "in terms of how important and malleable the brain is. If we take things away from kids, like their freedom, family support, the damage is almost on the level of taking things from an infant." The flip side of this is that they can easily change for the better as well. We just have to give them a chance.

Despite the existence of programs like the one in Toledo, the system as a whole does not support, encourage, or provide for these kids. The system is designed for them to fail.

The bogeyman is real. But it's us.

For every kid in the system, there are concentric circles of people affected—parents, siblings, children, community. Each one of these stories causes ripples. It rips families apart. The War on Drugs snatched the man out of the household, left Mom alone to raise the kids. "Nearly two-thirds of all black people in this country have a family member who has been to prison.... That's 2.7 million children who have a parent, at this very moment, sitting in a cage. Five million American children have lived this way."

At Luis Muñoz Marin Elementary School for Social Justice, in Newark, I sat in on a class run by visiting instructor Dr. Bahiyyah Muhammad from Howard University. One of the issues she addressed is that kids shouldn't be afraid to share their feelings on these issues, how their family situation has affected them, how they are dealing with it on the inside. Just about every kid in that class had a family member in the system. The kids were given a coloring book called *The Prison Alphabet* as a jumping-off point to start talking about these things, and then they shared essays they wrote about their personal experience. They are not usually encouraged to express these kinds of feelings, and there's a stigma that follows all of them around. We have to give them the opportunity and space to talk about it because if they keep it inside, it just festers. Black boys especially are taught from an early age to hide their feelings and keep them pushed down, that somehow this is what toughness means. But our vulnerability is how we get the strength to build back. *You can't heal what you never reveal.*

I met the most amazing kids in that school, kids who had light, kids who were hanging on to hope. Kids like Michael, a shy young eleven-year-old with a scar under his eye. When I sat down with him, he told me about people he had on the inside. It was heavy, and my instinct was to try to cheer him up, so I thought about how I could bring hope into this conversation. *Oh, I know!* I thought. *I'm going to ask him about his future.*

"So, what do you want to be when you grow up?" I asked.

Michael's answer? A Department of Youth and Family Services (DYFS) worker, so he could tell kids like himself "you can get through it because I got through it."

That was it for me; I broke down. I've learned how to be vulnerable on-camera—as someone else—but when it was really my own emotions, really me, I shooed the cameras away.

These were fifth and sixth graders talking like this. After a while you can go numb listening to all the stories, all the sadness, all the unfair hands they'd been dealt, but it's *imperative that we hear them.* They need to be heard. The trauma ages the kids. It takes their youth away, and they can't ever get that back. Like the enamel on your teeth.

We need to change the conversation, the knee-jerk reaction we have to kids who get tied up in the system. By setting these traps for them, we are responsible for their bad choices. Among the progressive programs I learned about in *Raised* is the Office of Neighborhood Safety (ONS) in Richmond, California, a city outside of Oakland that had a rising homicide rate in the years before the program started. ONS, then run by the inspiring DeVone Boggan, is an alternative program for at-risk kids that gives them ways to participate in violence intervention and community safety. They give fellowships to kids with violent pasts who can help recruit others to join, and then plan for their futures, pursue jobs, even get paid. In the years after the program started, the homicide rate in Richmond dropped *drastically.*

Sam, an ONS program coordinator who's in the film, told me that in their neighborhoods, nobody knows how to aspire to be a doctor or lawyer because they don't see that. They don't live where they see those things. And when those who do make it leave, they leave nothing behind. No breadcrumbs.

*Breadcrumbs.* That stuck with me.

# CHAPTER 16

# OUR KIDS

**GREEN HAVEN CORRECTIONAL FACILITY
STORMVILLE, NEW YORK
2017**

Dominic could've given up; he had every rea-son to. Twenty-five to life does that to people. But by focus-ing not on the bars around him but the self that was still free, he became a leader to a group of men who had nowhere else to turn. I went from being heartbroken for my nephew to being in awe of him.

It took some time but the Vice on HBO team got ap-proval from the New York State Bureau of Prisons to shoot not just in the visiting room at Green Haven but in Dom's cell, as well as in the class he taught for a program called Exodus, which he'd helped to bring to the prison. It was the first time in twenty years I got to see Dom inside those walls, to see who he had become. After all that time many men in prison have a stack of tickets—disciplinary incidents—but when I went to Dominic's cell, he showed me a folder of certificates and awards. I got to see my nephew in his element, feel the respect and love he got from others. It told me everything about the man he had become.

Virtually everyone in Dom's program had been in the system since they were teenagers. Grown men, some lifers, some in middle age, were talking about strategies they learned from "Tyson" (Dom's nickname), about getting to the root of their emotions, about changing the way they responded to situations, about loving themselves. These were lessons someone should have taught them from a young age. It was like traveling to the other end of the juvenile justice line and feeling hope that things didn't have to be this way.

Based on Dom's long list of commendations, the superintendent of Green Haven had recommended Dom for clemency the year before filming, but he didn't receive it. The next year, he recommended Dom again. At some point, talking to Dave Laven and Matt Horowitz, who shared directing duties on the film, I started wondering, *Damn, wouldn't it be something if my nephew came out of prison and we got that on film?*

And that's exactly what happened.

Dom's commutation and early release by Governor Cuomo at the end of 2017 served as the climax of the film. Right there on-camera, he steps out of Green Haven, looking like a new man in a fresh dark suit. In the car he turns to me and says, "I'm ready . . . I'm ready to make an impact on the community in a very, very positive way." We were able to end the film on an uplifting note, saying to the viewer: *These people are not done. They have lives to lead. A contribution to make. The work continues.*

The work continues.

Dom taught me it starts with our mindset. We change our thinking and find ways to execute our vision from there. When he came home, I got to see the man he had become. In prison he had educated himself, bringing dignity back to the phrase "correctional facility." When he got out, he could have just coasted and lived a quiet life. He'd earned it. But that's not what he was about; he wanted to go back in.

DAVID SIMON WAS GRACIOUS enough to co-host the premiere of *Raised in the System* at the Whitby Hotel in midtown Manhattan, where we had the press, bright lights, red carpet, and all that. It was beautiful to see Sam and Deandre, a program coordinator and a member from the Office of Neighborhood Safety in Richmond, at the screening, which also included a Q&A with author and activist Wes Moore.

Vice and HBO did their thing for the rollout of *Raised*, but there's only so much money and attention any company is going to put on one project. So once that all fizzled out, I looked at Dominic.

"Are you ready?" I asked.

"Right with you, Unc. Let's do it."

We started doing our own screenings, raising and using our own money to keep this thing going, with the help of a social justice advocate named Dana Rachlin. Dana founded NYC Together, which began as an alternative-to-suspension program operating inside schools, elevating the voices of young people directly impacted by overpolicing. NYC Together supports overpoliced and other impacted youth, helping them get the things they need and position them as problem solvers in their own communities.

I remember having a conversation with Dana right before *Raised* was released. I was excited about showing it around my old stomping grounds and other communities of color most affected by the issues. My plan was to bring the film to the hood.

"That's great, Mike," Dana said in her thick Staten Island accent, which is the most New York thing on the planet. "Show it to people who come from places like Vanderveer. But listen: it's important to also screen it for people who *don't*. You want to reach those in rooms of power, who are in positions to help. Cops need to see this, judges need to see this, lawyers need to see this." She made the point that when we go to juvenile facilities, the adults who need to see the film would have to be in the room anyway to supervise the kids, so we'd be bringing them both together around this issue. I credit Dana with helping me realize that making *Raised* wasn't the final product; it was just the beginning.

We teamed up for screenings around New York and around the country, generating discussion around criminal justice, juvenile justice, policing, and community safety, but also catalyzing action. We invited activists, advocates, artists, law enforcement, and of course community members directly affected by these issues, especially young people.

At the screenings, Dom would be in the audience, and when the film ended, we'd bring him up onstage to deafening applause. *Deafening*. Even police officers cheered. The audience was applauding his freedom but also what he chose to *do* with that freedom. "When I was coming up in my teenage years and going to prison," Dom said at a Brooklyn screening, "these types of conversations were not happening in my community."

We screened in places like Rikers Island and NYU and all places in between, like the Brooklyn Museum and Carnegie Hall's Weill Music Institute, where we had young Black mentees working with the Department of Probation leading the discussion. We took it to police academies, prisons, juvenile facilities. Dana is a warrior, a fierce fighter who doesn't take shit, and she would become my ongoing partner in the work.

And through all these events, I didn't meet a single stranger along the way. Every kid I met reminded me of myself. The more and more people I met in the course of screening and discussing the film, the more the larger problem came into clearer focus.

It's not rocket science: they need us. And we have a duty to respond.

## CLEVELAND, OHIO, NOVEMBER 2018

We brought *Raised in the System* to a youth detention facility in Cleveland, where we showed the film in a classroom to kids whose voices still hadn't dropped, who didn't yet have hair on their bodies. There was a twelve-year-old boy at his desk who was so small that his blue uniform's sleeves and cuffs were rolled up to keep from falling down. He looked like a child in a man's costume, which is exactly what he was. Just watching him told me that something has gone horribly wrong with the justice system in this country. How can we have allowed this to happen?

After the film we held a discussion in the classroom. As with all kids, they were a little shy, but they slowly opened up. A thirteen-year-old white boy raised his hand. "Mr. Mike," he said, "can I ask a question?"

"Sure, man," I said. "That's why we're here."

"You think I'll ever be adopted?"

It was not what I expected. There was a pause as I made eye contact with the teacher, who was sitting at a desk in the middle of the room.

"Of course you will," I said, instinctively walking toward his desk. "Why would you ask that?" I thought of it as the kind of thing a scared kid just needed to hear: *Of course someone will adopt you.*

His eyes stayed glued to the floor. "'Cause every time they put me in a foster home they abuse me and then I fight back and they put me back here," he said. "Then that goes on my record and I look bad on the paper."

I was stunned into silence. This kid wasn't just insecure. He was reacting to the messages he was receiving. The system was criminalizing his response to abuse, punishing him for trying to protect himself. It must've felt like the world had given up on him.

At another desk was a light-skinned Black boy with deep-set eyes who was rubbing his head like an old man. "Sometimes, I don't know," he said later in our conversation. "I kind of feel like these walls are closing in on me." It was a haunting sentence from a thirteen-year-old. As I was processing where a child would learn to talk like this, what could cause him to feel that, he came back with the kicker: "You know, I just don't—I don't feel *loved*."

After those words hit the air, everyone in the room got real quiet. This heaviness just hung in that classroom. For lack of anything else to do, I walked over, wrapped my arms around him, and held him tight. "We're all gonna love on you. From now on," I said, "everyone in this room is gonna love on each other." I couldn't help wondering who the criminals were here. We were making children forget the concept of love.

Though I was only scheduled to talk to that one class, I went down the hall and dropped in on every classroom on that floor. I tried to give words of encouragement, remind them to be accountable for their actions, and tell them that people care about them, that we are here even when they can't see us. On our way out, one of the teachers, a Black woman around my age, told me she used to teach in the public school system. She realized that one of the boys in the class—the twelve-year-old whose body disappeared into his uniform—was actually the son of one of her former students. I could see the heaviness in her eyes as she told me this, knowing she taught the father and is now teaching the son behind bars. It drove home how cyclical the problems are.

We went from the detention center to another screening, at Cleveland-Marshall College of Law. This was part of Dana's plan to bring the film to the power holders. It made sense to try to reach law school students, men and women preparing to enter the legal system whose minds are still fertile and open. Hopefully, by the time they are in a position to make a difference, they'll be on the right side of this issue.

There's a coldness to the justice system, but at the root, it is only made up of people. And people have to see other people. The decision-makers in high offices need to see what's going on at the ground level. They have to feel the damage they're doing with these laws and policies because too many of them are insulated from it.

The environment on the college campus was so different from the detention center that it was like a whipsaw. As little as ten years separated the kids in detention from the law school students, but the gap seemed insurmountable. And though the students and professors seemed committed to remaining a force in the community, the disparities were overwhelming. Going from one to the other was intense, like a change in air pressure drastic enough to kill me.

Then we went to Edwins, the restaurant run by ex-felons, with the ACLU and the Innocence Project, and Daniel dropped that question on me that opens this book: "Mr. Michael . . . are you happy?"

The heaviness of the day was weighing on me, and it was after I'd had a couple glasses of red wine at Edwins that Daniel asked that question. I was not mentally or emotionally prepared for it, and I had guilt behind the drink because I knew better. As an addict, I should not have been drinking. For me it's the same as drugs, because your defenses break down. I was not an alcoholic in the way that "Earthlings"—non-addicts—think of it. But alcohol activates my blind spots and makes me forget. I know about the depths to which drugs have taken me, and alcohol literally makes me forget all that pain. So I'll feel safe. And then I'll get a bright idea.

The day had woken up my trauma, and that night after dinner, just walking around Cleveland, I felt myself starting to get that bright idea. I made it back to my hotel room and looked out my window, staring at the city and thinking about going out there and scoring some crack, finding some way to numb the pain. Through a mix of grace and stubborn will, I managed to get through the night without getting high. But I have to keep my guard up. I know it always comes back around; you're never free for good.

AS PART OF THE work around social- and criminal-justice issues, Dana Rachlin began hosting "salons," or social justice dinners, where she'd invite a whole mix of people to break bread together: high-ranking law enforcement, formerly incarcerated men and women, artists and influencers, experts on particular issues, and young people from the community.* We'd all eat together, family style, at a big table in the back of a restaurant. The key was that the young people were not there for us to lecture to; the point was to let them take the lead. They're almost never in the rooms where decisions are made that affect them most directly, and by empowering them we make it more likely they'll stay involved. We cannot forget that those closest to the problem are closest to the solution.

The conversations were raw but healing, full of gut-wrenching honesty. For a lot of people at that table it was the

* Shout-out to Shani Kulture of Hot 97, who partnered with us for this (and future initiatives) and offered his restaurant for the first dinner.

first time they'd sat down in settings like that, across from a police officer, especially a high-ranking one. There were so many moments that gave me hope, but one in particular stands out. At the end of a dinner one of the young men, a football player kind of dude, said, "Next time we have to get some LGBTQ, transgenders up in here. Their voice counts too."

I was like, *Goddamn, we are getting somewhere with this.*

One of the early dinners included Edwin Raymond, a police officer who has been trying to rip the cover off of the NYPD's overpolicing of poor neighborhoods of color, sacrificing himself to change the way police interact with these communities. When I met him, I felt like I found another brother. The heart on this man, a Brooklyn Caribbean man like me, the light he shines, is just blinding. He's almost regal, with his dark skin and head of long dreadlocks. Being around him and seeing what he's been doing has been an inspiration.

I developed other relationships with the NYPD, reached out to partner with community members, got friends from the industry to contribute so this thing we had going could expand and regenerate itself. Raising money for new programs at NYC Together, as well as for my own nonprofit Making Kids Win, was something I knew I could do. Dana helped me with getting my mind around going into these rooms and asking for help.

"Michael," she'd say, "stop acting like we're asking them for anything special for our kids in these communities. We're not. We take out all the resources, replace it with unhealthy shit, and we ask these already fragile adolescents to perform, make healthy choices and decisions."

"No, no, you're right," I'd say, "I'm just—"

"Do not let them off the hook, Michael. *Do not.*" I promised her I wouldn't.

WE CANNOT BE WHAT *we cannot see.* Around this time, a friend of mine had to drop out at the last minute of a talk with teenagers about motivation and focus. As quickly as we could, Edwin, Jim St. Germain (another West Indian boy made good who I met through Dana), and I went over there to fill in. The event was at an alternative school in Brooklyn, ACORN Community High School, where five successful Black men from Brooklyn stood at the front of the room. That alone made me proud. And the kids in the audience sat quiet, attentive. There was not one yawn or outburst: these kids were hungry for change. *They saw themselves in us.*

When we were done talking, they came forward and crowded around, asked questions, and we traded some phone numbers. They all wanted a copy of Jim's book, *A Stone of Hope,* a memoir about his time in the system and the work he's been doing to lift others up and advocate to raise the age of criminal responsibility. His book was a hook for them, a way in. I've seen the power of reading and the desire to hear these stories, and for a time I found myself giving copies of Jim's book out to every kid I saw. Jim was saved by a couple of parental figures, a dinner table, and a few books. Like I always say: *This is not rocket science.* We know what these kids need. Just to be seen. And loved. And told they matter. For some kids it takes just one adult to care about them, take an interest in them. Once you get activated by that idea, it makes it damn near impossible to turn your back on any single one of them.

AFTER I GOT BACK from that Ohio trip, Daniel and I stayed in touch. After losing his mother at four and his best friend at thirteen, he has lost six more friends to violence and many others to jail. He was seventeen years old, not even out of high school, staring down the kind of trauma that most old men don't ever have to face.

I could see Daniel was trying to make a break from the old life, so I wanted to be there for him. He was teetering and maybe I could be an inflection point. I wanted to give him what the arts community, my mother, Robin, the Hill brothers, and Reverend Ron gave to me. Love and a link to somewhere else. The possibility of something else.

We need a revolution of the spirit to change these kids' stories. Daniel has an old soul, and he talks about his young life as though he were looking back on fifty years. I'll call to check in with him or he'll ring me just to talk, even to check up on me. He's got a good heart and isn't selfish either; one time I sent him new kicks and he sold them to put food in his auntie's refrigerator.

It's heartbreaking, as an adult who has been spared the worst of the darkness, to see how we normalize this trauma and dysfunction in the community. In the twenty-first century, in the richest, most powerful country on Earth, we're making young kids forget the concept of love. Or making sure they never know it in the first place. That should be unacceptable to all of us.

My job as an actor, as an entertainer, can't be its own thing anymore. I've been activated and stimulated, and now I have to learn how to harmonize my two worlds. In the past I might have compartmentalized my selves, found ways out of dealing with the messiness that comes with paying attention.

*You want to eat? Read the line.*

*You want to get kicked out of the business? Speak your mind.*

I'm done with it. I can't go back to work with the same blinders on.

# CHAPTER 17

# THE WORK

ATLANTA, GEORGIA
2019

EVERY ROLE I TAKE ON TAKES A PIECE OUT OF ME. Some take a bigger chunk than others. Through the years I've learned how to go there, but only recently am I learning how to come back. Konstantin Stanislavski, who invented in acting what became known as the Method, taught that you're not supposed to use unaddressed trauma for your craft. You have to address it *before* it can become a tool for art. I had read that years ago, but I am only really starting to understand it now.

I had been using the arts as a way to escape from rather than deal with my issues. As a result, the characters that I played were getting closer and closer to the white meat. By scratching at these unresolved issues, I was bringing it all to the surface but not addressing it. That's usually when I'd end up getting those bright ideas.

In Atlanta, shooting the HBO series *Lovecraft Country*

put me through the wringer, mentally and emotionally. For one, it brought up something new for me: generational trauma. These were things I didn't even know I carried, things that have traveled in my DNA. My character, Montrose Freeman, is a closeted Black man who is a product of Jim Crow and a survivor of the 1921 Tulsa Race Massacre. Playing him connected me to the collective trauma that's been visited upon Black America, the world that created my world. The why of the world I was raised in and still live in. It wasn't just a history lesson for me; it was more immediate and urgent than that. Present. As I said to a friend at the time, "The ancestors are visiting me in my work."

Montrose's strained relationship with his son is central to the story, which dug up issues with my own father, who passed on in 2010. Montrose, my father, and I were all drilled with those lessons about Black masculinity and toughness, about wearing a mask to hide our vulnerabilities. Playing Montrose also gave me perspective on my mother, allowing me to reach a place of forgiveness. I honestly feel like she did the best she could with the situation she was dealt.

In hindsight, I can see how I needed to go through all that, how I've come out the other end stronger, but as it was happening, it was scary. I had no support system down in Atlanta, so I went to my old standby. As I've said many times before: Drugs are not the problem. Drugs are a symptom of the problem.

I learned that I don't get to shortcut my way around doing the work. Even though I was using my pain, channeling it into the arts, that doesn't really count. That's not the work. The work requires you to look in the mirror, and you can't do that until you put the drugs down. When I got back from Atlanta, I got into therapy and Narcotics Anonymous meetings, reconnected with my sponsor, and addressed my trauma head-on. I've accepted that I cannot let up. I've got to do the personal work so I can do the professional work, which is where I get the platform to do the real work. It's all connected. I have to clear my baggage first so I can walk into my blessing and claim my stage so I can do what I was intended to do: the purpose-driven life. Be a beacon of life for the youth.

Back when I was living in Vanderveer, going on auditions before the years of *The Wire*, I took side streets to avoid Flatbush Avenue traffic into Manhattan, which took me past the Brooklyn Navy Yard. I had heard a rumor that Robert De Niro was looking to turn the area into a Hollywood studio. "This is great," I said. "I don't have to move to Cali to become an actor! I can do it right from home. And I even got a name for it: Hollyhood!" I was dead serious. "This is perfect. I can stay home. I already even have my route to get to work."*

For years after that, I would look back and laugh. I saw everything, I visualized *everything* except leaving my neighborhood. I used to tell that story as a knock against me, an example of how shortsighted I was. I could see this entire future—being on TV and in movies, being a success, but I couldn't see myself getting out of the hood. Not that long ago, I was telling that story for the thousandth time when it

* That exact thing came to fruition on *Boardwalk Empire*, which was shot on a giant lot in Greenpoint, Brooklyn.

hit me. Wait a minute: I wasn't shortsighted. I had *vision*. Even in my dreams, I stayed here. I kept myself here for a reason.

Why's all this focus on getting out? How come people from my community, when we find success, are taught and programmed to leave the community that made us successful? That's backwards. If I'm not leaving breadcrumbs, then what is all this for? Brooklyn made me who I am, so why would I not come back and share my successes with the kids in my community? That's never going to change.

People like to pull me aside at community events and say things like, "I just want to tell you that you're doing such a good thing."

"Stop that," I say. "Change that narrative. I am doing nothing special. This is the normal. All I did was come home."

WHEN I BECAME AN actor and Hollywood was looking to me to create certain stories, I didn't worry about being typecast. "Typecast?" I would answer when people asked me about that. "Hell no, I was worried about not eating." But it's become more than that. I wear it as a badge of honor that I get to portray these people, inhabit these roles. These are my people. It's a privilege to tell their stories, to bring their humanity forward to those who see themselves in the characters and to those who *don't*. I want them to leave feeling understanding, compassion, empathy. It doesn't mean agreeing, excusing it, or liking it at all: it just means *one human being seeing another human being*. Really seeing them, not just taking a quick look and thinking they know. If someone asked me to describe the common thread in all that I do—my mission in acting, producing, community, and even just my living day-to-day—that's it.

In getting a part in Ava DuVernay's series on the Exonerated Five, *When They See Us*, I got a close-up look at how much damage the system has wrought. The series tells the true story of five Black and Brown kids in New York City who were falsely accused of raping and beating a white woman in Central Park in 1989. The five young teenagers supposedly "confessed" to the crimes, though police and prosecutorial misconduct in the case was rampant. The story made national news in 1989—around the time I was in rehab—and I remember it well. Any Black man of a certain age around that period in New York thought about how easily that could've been him. Wrong place, wrong time, wrong color. It can happen just like that.

Because of a dishonest police force and shortsighted lawyers who didn't give a damn about justice, each of the five young men spent years behind bars until the real culprit's confession and DNA test freed them. The boys' lives were upended, and their imprisonment rippled into their families and communities at large. When they got out, they had lost their childhood and had to put their lives back together in a city that had thrown them away. The injustice of what happened to them, the way a whole system, a whole *city*, railroaded them, should haunt all of us. The series portrays each of the Exonerated Five not just as headlines or victims, but as the individual and beautiful souls they are.

Spending time with the actual Exonerated Five—Korey Wise, Yusaaf Salaam, Raymond Santana, Kevin Richardson, and Antron McCray (whose father I play in the series)— I was touched by their humanity, their graciousness, and their refusal to be defined by their anger. We've broken bread and I'm grateful to have gotten to know them, but my heart hurts for the ways their experience must have traumatized them. We're all teetering, some closer to the edge than others, which is why it's imperative we reach out both ahead and behind, grab on to someone, let them know we're here and that we see them. That's why the series is called *When They See Us*. That recognition is so simple but so vital. I know its power. I'm still here because of its power.

I understand these characters. I've seen their journey. I knew why Bobby McCray made that fateful decision to let his son sign that false confession, about the guilt he carried, about the reason he had to pull away from his family. The Exonerated Five's story is among the most famous, but it's a well-worn template. When injustices and mistakes compound and compound and compound on the same group of people, they start to look a lot less like mistakes. They look like a plan.

At a press event for *When They See Us*, Ava DuVernay made that point. "Let's not pretend for a moment that this system is broken," she said. "It is working properly. It is doing exactly what it is designed to do." The kids are deprived, sorted, and discarded and then are forced to make poor choices based on that circumstance. It's not the other way around; they don't choose first.

We make the first move. It starts with us.

## BROWNSVILLE, NEW YORK, MARCH 2020

One afternoon right before the COVID-19 pandemic hit the States, I was with Dana Rachlin in Brownsville, a neighborhood in Brooklyn that has long been one of the poorest and most violent areas of the city. I remember trips there with my mother when I was young, back when it was a vibrant and beautiful community. The years had been hard on the neighborhood. Dana was going out there for a meeting and I decided to tag along, for really no reason at all. Which was kind of the point.

Dana had been talking about the captain at the local seventy-third precinct as someone I should meet, so we went by the police department. At the entrance, Dana flipped her hair and walked right through the metal detectors like it was no big thing. That's Dana. But I froze: I was fifty-three years old and I had never in my life walked into a police station like that, never felt welcome to do so. I was wearing a kilt over sweatpants and hesitated, thinking, "Uh, don't they want to search me or something?"

Dana saw I wasn't passing through and turned back to me. "Michael, what are you doing?" she asked.

I wasn't sure. What the hell *was* I doing?

We walked through the precinct past the desks of cops doing their daily work, and I couldn't shake this anxiety just being there. It felt strange. That feeling dissipated a bit when Dana introduced me to Capt. Derby St. Fort, a Haitian man in his late thirties. Anytime I see a dark-skinned man, especially from an island immigrant background, it affects me profoundly. It means something to me to see a brother like that in a crisp white shirt and badge, in a position of authority.

Captain St. Fort had kind eyes and this gentle soul that, to me, felt very un-coplike. He told me about the change in culture and policing that was coming to Brownsville, how they were working to reimagine public safety. "We're trying to involve community-based organizations and violence interrupters to address the issues in Brownsville," he said. Violence interrupters are formerly incarcerated people, credible messengers, who disrupt violence brewing in the community. Those who have been to prison, who once ran in gangs, are able to get through to young people who maybe won't listen to anyone else. The violence interrupters want to become part of the solution; all we have to do is let them. It became clear as we talked that Captain St. Fort had all these answers to questions posed by the hood, that he was a revolutionary in uniform, but the higher-ups weren't listening.

Then Dana and I strolled the blocks of Brownsville with the captain. We spoke with residents, met with violence interrupters, went into businesses, stopped by community-based organizations like Brownsville Community Justice Center and Collective Fare, which feeds the community while also teaching restaurant skills to teens and others looking for work.

The amount of love I received on that street was overwhelming.

"You don't understand," one of the cops said to me. "No one comes here. No one like you comes back here. Ever."

I stopped feeling good about myself. We pay lip service to

the community, but do we ever spend time there? Do we get to know the people and remain a presence in their lives? I'm as guilty as anyone; I have to make my return to the neighborhood less of an event and more of a habit. It was like I was staring at a problem that I also represented. That day was one of the first times I walked around the hood in an informal setting like that, just being connected to the work and the people. I did events and visited Vanderveer, but what about just going back for no reason at all?

We passed blocks of boarded-up and abandoned buildings that just broke my heart. "It's crazy," I said.

"What is?" Dana asked.

"When I was a kid, this was a thriving block. My mom used to get her wigs over there and then we'd go to the fish market. People from all over Brooklyn, from all over the *city*, used to get their fish in that one spot."

Captain St. Fort was telling me about the quality-of-life issues in the neighborhood and how they need to offer the youth more services. Then it hit me. I knew what I could do.

"This is where Making Kids Win should be," I said. "Why can't we get one of these plots?"

Making Kids Win (MKW), a nonprofit I started, is dedicated to safe spaces in the community for kids to learn and play and just be kids. I know how hard the simplest things are when the options in your neighborhood are so limited. With the help of some professionals, I developed a plan and went about executing it. The plan with MKW was to address community issues through two initiatives: one based off of ONS in Richmond, dedicated to reducing gun violence and the related deaths and incarceration of community youth, and another modeled off of Urban Arts Partnership, working to engage youth in the arts as an outlet and possible career path.

There's so much potential—and untapped power—that never gets to see the light of day in these communities. It is smothered and squashed before it has a chance to breathe and grow. If I was going to try to cultivate it, why not do it here, in a neighborhood that bears the brunt of public policy and cuts to city funding? We would try to stake a small claim and make it grow into something meaningful. In Brownsville that day, I was uplifted, but I was also shamed. I hadn't been *home*. We can't leave our kids to be raised by just these strong women and police. The men have to be there too, contribute, be visual.

"Thank you, sir," I told Captain St. Fort as we left. "It's like I had forgotten I'm from Brooklyn."

A month or so later, when Brownsville got hit extra hard by both COVID and police violence, we returned to hand out PPE, educate residents on safety and wellness during the pandemic, and to lift people up. We'd return again and again.

Brownsville isn't where I live, but it *is* my home. I know these people. I see myself in every inch of this community. I know about getting dressed up, matching shoes to jacket to hang on the corner. Returning to what I call "the scene of the crime"—the makings of who I am—is imperative. It's about life and death, my life and death. If my community is gone, where am I going to go?

**PITTSBURGH, PENNSYLVANIA**
**NOVEMBER 2020**

That fall, I got a call from Daniel that he was graduating from TIP, the Trade Institute of Pittsburgh. No way on earth I was going to miss that, so my friend Jermaine and I flew out there. It was a ghost town, with much of the city still in the depths of COVID-19 and most of the world still in lockdown.

After the ceremony, Jermaine and I went out to a steakhouse with Daniel, his friend, and Daniel's father. At some point at the dinner, Daniel took out his phone and showed me an Instagram page for blocks in Cleveland that tells you who has been murdered recently on the streets. (There's one in Baltimore too.) If you haven't seen or heard from one of your boys, you look them up on there to see if their death is posted.

"Let me see if any of my homies on the page today," Daniel said. The way he opened up that page so nonchalantly, scrolling like we do on Facebook or Twitter, was shocking. Jermaine and I met each other's eyes across the table. We were just floored. How could this be happening? Talk about normalizing the abnormal. My heart bleeds for Daniel, for all the friends he lost, but what makes it bleed even more is how *normal* it has become for him. It's so accepted that the method we use to share our celebrations and successes is how his generation is sharing their dead. Even on his graduation day, this was what this young man was carrying. The contrast stood out to me, but it didn't to him. He was used to it.

Almost immediately, Daniel pulled up a video that showed paramedics trying to resuscitate someone on the sidewalk. When it ended, he was trying to play it off like no big deal. "It's all good," he said.

"What? No!" I said. "This is not normal. It's not 'all good,' not at all, man."

Daniel and his friend were processing this heaviness the only way they knew how.

"Listen," I said, "you have to stay the course so you do not end up like that. You have to finish what you started."

More and more, I'm realizing how abnormal my own normal was, and these kids are still living it. I want to introduce them to some new normalcy. That way we can start talking about and dealing with the trauma instead of acting like it's "all good"—which it never is. We have another generation of young Black men so grown before their time, and though there are major structural things that need to be done about poverty and systemic racism, we also have to be okay talking about it, putting it all out there. If not, they'll never be able to get out from under it.

# CHAPTER 18

# COMING HOME

*Service simply means we embrace the
possibility of living for more than
ourselves. . . . I'm convinced that most
of the time, that's what the voice inside
of us is telling us to do. To live for more
than ourselves.*

—Wes Moore

**BROOKLYN, NEW YORK**
**2020**

AS I'VE BEEN WORKING ON THIS BOOK, THE WORLD
has been changing before our very eyes. I'm doing what I can
to keep my two feet in it and my ear to the ground. We're at
an inflection point that goes beyond anything we've seen before. What began years ago with Trayvon Martin's murder,
then Eric Garner's and Michael Brown's, and recently, Bre-
onna Taylor's and George Floyd's, has swelled into a movement too loud for even the most comfortable to tune out.
The ground is ripe for change. This moment can't just pass us

by. We need to grab it with both hands, hold tight, and—no matter what the world tries to drop on us—refuse to let go.

After COVID-19 hit, New York City gutted all of the youth summer programs in the city, and those of us who cared about the community knew we had to step in. New York was an epicenter of the pandemic, and Brown and Black neighborhoods were the epicenter of the epicenter, so we started to look at what we could do to get in there and help. The murder rate always goes up when school lets out in the summer, and with a pandemic that was ruining lives and livelihoods, things were bound to be even worse.

*When white people catch a cold,* they say, *Black people get pneumonia.* Whatever crises happen in society hit a thousand times worse in the hood. When budget shortfalls come down, they always come down hardest there. The mayor canceled summer camp and youth employment programs, which fund healthy summer experiences and paying jobs for the poorest kids in the city. At the same time, the city has increased police presence in those same communities. Taking away things for them to do and then adding cops was a recipe for disaster.

In the park near my neighborhood in Williamsburg, where I've been running, the bathrooms are open and sanitized. Four miles from my place, in Brownsville, they've got shackles and chains on those same doors and have blocked off the playground. These kids can't even get into their park; there are no backyards or lawns they can go to. They hang outside their buildings and then the police want to come in and crack skulls.

For summer 2020, I worked with Dana and NYC Together on instituting Project LEAD: Learn, Earn, Advocate, Deliver. It was a summer youth employment program that offered a healthy outlet for young men and women at a time when their options were limited. We raised money so Project LEAD could hire teens to come up with their own campaign around social distancing and messaging about the pandemic in Black and Brown communities. The idea is to let them lead—it's their generation; it's their voice. They're the ones to whom we should be handing the keys.

I grew up in a household where a child was to be seen and not heard. I'm beginning to unlearn that. These kids are growing up faster than we did, have been exposed to more, and are not as naïve as we once were. You can see it; this generation is different, and they're tired of the bullshit. The things that tear apart the adults—race, sexual orientation, religion, identity—don't seem to bother them as much, if at all. They're focused on big-picture things, like making sure the Earth doesn't kick us off it. Those coming of age carry a different energy, and they are going to bring change—whether it's Greta Thunberg in Sweden working on climate change or Parkland, Florida, shooting survivor X González working on gun violence. I've seen it at the ground level. To watch the lights go on in these children's eyes, to see them empowered, is everything to me.

I've learned a lot these past few years in interacting with the youth, who are savvy and can smell your BS a mile away. I've found the best way to enter their orbit is by asking and listening. "What do you all think?" I ask. "Tell me what's going on." I do that over and over again, and I find I have a better shot of slipping past their defenses and getting in.

You have to navigate carefully—guide without instructing. They're hungry to take action but don't want to be told how—especially by those who are *responsible* for the problems. I hear from them, and there's some of that positive rebellious energy: *You can't tell me a damn thing; you're the ones who fucked it all up in the first place.*

They're not wrong.

WHEN THE SUMMER WAS over and COVID was still an issue, NYC Together shifted to a new program, We Build the Block. What began with those social-justice dinners around the time of *Raised in the System* had expanded into a campaign for large-scale policy ideas along with voter and civic engagement. We Build the Block hired youth organizers to go out there and mobilize, educate, and register voters. The name that was given to those young men and women was Crew Count.

The name Crew Count was a response to Operation Crew Cut, which was an NYPD program that collected the names of some forty thousand teens (and adults) in gangs—many "loosely affiliated" with gangs, as in they lived on certain blocks or in certain buildings—then put them on surveillance and in gang databases without their knowledge. Experts found that the massive expansion led to "threats, surveillance and harassment."

We Build the Block threw block parties—called block activations—in the most overpoliced areas, neighborhoods with the most community members who were formerly incarcerated. We paid all local food vendors, DJs, and musicians, and brought in Crew Count to inform residents on the issues and register them to vote, even sometimes bringing candidates onto the block. It was a way of saying to those in power that these voters matter because they're most affected by your policies. *Talk to them.*

In my community, I still cannot believe how many adults don't vote or think voting doesn't matter. If you are a person of color in a community like I'm from and think like that, then I'm sorry, but you are part of the problem. There's no excuse to be ignorant anymore. The price of being ignorant is they get to use our ignorance against us.

We didn't have any police at the block activations because overpolicing was one of the issues we were trying to address. We had the OGs of the block running security, and nothing was going down without their say-so. It was a way to say we take care of our own. "We'll call you when we need you," we'd tell the cops. "Right now, we don't need you policing us." That's part of the problem—the cops hovering over us, waiting for someone to look sideways. In all our block activations, there was not one single incident of violence whatsoever.

Older residents were coming up to me in shock, saying, "We haven't had a block party for ten years." Ten years! It warmed my heart, reminding me of the jams we had in the courtyards of Vanderveer and the larger summer parties we later had after blocking off Foster Avenue. Those are some of the happiest memories I have. We were bringing all that back, that culture, that feeling of togetherness in the community, but now with a political-action component.

In June 2021, right before the Democratic mayoral primary, almost all the major candidates came and got put in the hot seat at our block activation in Brownsville. We let our youth talk to them, question them, engage in a dialogue on the issues that most affect them. It was meaningful and powerful, seeing these kids lead.

With We Build the Block we're creating a model, and the goal is to ultimately take it around New York City and then to cities all over the country. It's a movement. These entrenched problems need to be dealt with at the root level. We can't wait for people to invite us to the table. We have to build our own table. If you're waiting for them—whoever they are—you're holding your breath. *There's no justice,* they say. *There's just us.* And if we each do our part, that should be more than enough.

One young man I met, a thicker boy with dark skin, had this infectious spirit. He saw what we were doing with We Build the Block and he said, "I wanna do one on my block," which happened to be the worst block in Brownsville. And he did it. He was able to galvanize the community, under Dana's tutelage, and got us down there to do an activation, and then he ran the interviews of the candidates. These are not eighteen-year-olds heading off to Harvard to "do good and do well"; they are staying in their community.

I'm finally starting to do the same. I go in there apologizing for being absent in the community, not telling them how to be. There's no "I did it; you can do it" type of nonsense. I'm asking to be a part of their lives. I spent a lot of time away; but I tell them *I'm here now, what do you all need? Talk to me.*

I hate that feeling that they're thanking me—we're doing nothing special. I'm coming home. If I'm not returning to and investing in my community, what am I doing?

At the core of my work is service. Getting a second chance at life is about service. Wanting to use my time and platform to give back keeps me sane, keeps me balanced. It's part of my food now. It gives me perspective and purpose.

We have to get back to the idea of the village, figure out how to mend our struggling families in the community. Give them culture, respect, connection, the experience of dreaming and hoping. The permission to dream is so important. The permission to love yourself is so important. You don't have to get scarred up in your face and go through endless rehabs and almost die and overdose to finally understand that you're worth something.

The arts, when I took it on as a career, was a form of rebellion—from dance onward. I watched Janet Jackson dance on my television and thought maybe there was a chance I could make it. I never thought I would make it this far. It's like I was shoving my shoulder into a door never expecting it to open up, and then I fell into the room.

As I write this, I'm working with Vice to finish up Season 2 of *Black Market*. I was proud of the first season, but I was green, didn't know what I needed to know. We didn't go far enough, and I insisted that if we were going to do it again, we'd have to include some move toward redemption or resolution in each episode. I refuse to be a tourist in these worlds.

We'd lost a few people who were in Season 1, including that young gunrunner in Chicago who asked me to take him with me. That fact alone didn't sit right with me; we couldn't just drop in, film them, and leave. Season 2 has the redemption angle, whether it's introducing one of the subjects to someone who can help them or directing their skill sets in a legal way. We did an episode with credit card scammers, and I insisted that we shoot a scene with the current scammers meeting a reformed scammer. He talks to them about how to start an LLC, a way to do something legitimate with their money. It spoke to my larger journey, about coming back home and bringing something positive with me.

AT AROUND FIFTY YEARS old, I figured out who I am. But now I have to figure out *why I am*. I made it, great, now what? What was it for? I thought the destination was one thing but found it was another. If my shoulders aren't strong enough for others to stand on, then I'm wasting my second chance.

It has continued to bother me that the marker of success is "getting out." Where am I going? What does it say to the youth who are still here? To the adults who are raising them? What am I communicating by leaving?

Where are my breadcrumbs?

I need to use what was given to me to bring others up. I don't want to be in the spotlight, I want to *be the spotlight itself*. Shine on others. If you've got the light and the heat, it may stroke your ego, but so what? What are you going to do with it?

I can see it so clearly now. It's not about getting out. It never was. It's all about being welcomed back home.

# ACKNOWLEDGMENTS

Special thanks to Matt Goldman; Dominic Dupont; Dana Rachlin; Greg Cally; David Laven; Jermaine Ridgway; Goli Samii; Jerry Ricciotti; Michael Skolnik; Ray Thomas; Michael Kevin Darnall; Capt. Derby St. Fort; Matt Mahurin; Marcus Hill; Sue Kwon; Dr. Laurence Steinberg; David Simpkins; Lt. Edwin Raymond; Staci Dupont; Justin Gricus; Kevin Manahan; Matt Horowitz; Lyle Kendrick; Susanna Schwartz; Abby Wallace; Lydia Sternfeld; our agents, Susan Golomb and Wendy Sherman; Callie Deitrick; Mariah Stovall; Madeline Ticknor; our editor, Madhulika Sikka; Aubrey Martinson; Robert Siek; Gillian Blake; and everyone at Crown.

# LIST OF
# ORGANIZATIONS

NYC Together: nyctogether.org

We Build the Block/Crew Count: webuildtheblock.org

Urban Arts Partnership: urbanarts.org

The Soze Agency (Michael Skolnik's organization): wearesoze.com

Edwins Leadership and Restaurant Institute: edwinsrestaurant.org

Vice on HBO: *Raised in the System:* hbo.com/vice/season-06/raised
  -in-the-system

Brownsville Safety Alliance: millionexperiments.com/Brownsville
  -Safety-Alliance

Office of Neighborhood Safety (Richmond, CA): ci.richmond.ca.us
  /271/Office-of-Neighborhood-Safety

Advance Peace (Oakland, CA): advancepeace.org

The Marshall Project: themarshallproject.org

City Weeds (Baltimore): cityweedsbaltimore.com

We March On (Atlanta): actionnetwork.org/events/mo4vr-atl

The Innocence Project: innocenceproject.org

American Civil Liberties Union (ACLU): aclu.org

# NOTES

SIX: STRUNG

77    **"Those on the pipe"** David Simon and Ed Burns, *The Corner: A Year in the Life of an Inner-City Neighborhood* (New York: Broadway Books, 1997), 26.

ELEVEN: OMAR

153   **life expectancy in the Black neighborhoods** Matthew Horace, *The Black and the Blue: A Cop Reveals the Crimes, Racism, and Injustice in America's Law Enforcement* (New York: Legacy Lit, 2018), 59.

TWELVE: HIDING OUT IN NEWARK

160   **"A man gotta live"** "Know Your Place," *The Wire,* Season 4, Episode 9, original air date, November 12, 2006, written by Kia Corthron.

THIRTEEN: INFLUENCE

180   **"Not my favorite *person*"** J. Patrick Coolican, "Obama Goes Gloves Off, Head-On," *Las Vegas Sun,* January 14, 2008.

FIFTEEN: VOICE

201 **"Remember what they say"** Glenn E. Martin is credited with popularizing this phrase.

203 **"When African American children act out"** Paul Butler, *Chokehold: Policing Black Men* (New York: The New Press, 2017), 44.

204 **"spending a total of $5 billion"** Nell Bernstein, *Burning Down the House: The End of Juvenile Prison* (New York: The New Press, 2014), 13.

204 **You are thirty-eight times more likely** Bernstein, *Burning Down the House*, 13.

206 **"Harmless White fun"** Ibram X. Kendi, *How to Be an Anti-racist* (New York: One World, 2019), 204.

211 **"young people are far more likely"** Bernstein, *Burning Down the House*, 53.

211 **"Even in large, state-run"** Ibid.

211 **"*increasing* the odds that they will commit"** Bernstein, *Burning Down the House*, 10.

214 **They can't make better choices** This comes from Dr. Larry Steinberg, who told me, "We talk about their choices, but we don't talk about how constrained those choices are."

215 **car insurance is so high** Jeff Larson, et al., "How We Examined Racial Discrimination in Auto Insurance Prices," ProPublica, April 5, 2017.

216 **"Nearly two-thirds of all black people"** Jonathan Reuben Miller, *Halfway Home: Race, Punishment, and the Afterlife of Mass Incarceration* (New York: Little, Brown, 2021), 143.

SEVENTEEN: THE WORK

241 **a neighborhood that bears the brunt** Saki Knafo, "Bridging the Divide Between the Police and the Policed," *The New Yorker*, April 28, 2021.

EIGHTEEN: COMING HOME

244    **"Service simply means"** Wes Moore, *The Work: Searching for a Life That Matters* (New York: Spiegel & Grau, 2015), xxi.

247    **"threats, surveillance and harassment"** Stephon Johnson, "New Report Takes Anti-Gang Initiative 'Operation Crew Cut' to Task," *New York Amsterdam News,* December 12, 2019.

# PHOTO CREDITS